An Island in the Stream

An Island in the Stream

Ecocritical and Literary Responses to Cuban Environmental Culture

Edited by David Taylor, Scott Slovic,
and Armando Fernandez Soriano

LEXINGTON BOOKS
Lanham • Boulder • New York • London

Published by Lexington Books
An imprint of The Rowman & Littlefield Publishing Group, Inc.
4501 Forbes Boulevard, Suite 200, Lanham, Maryland 20706
www.rowman.com

6 Tinworth Street, London SE11 5AL

British Library Cataloguing in Publication Information Available

Library of Congress Cataloging-in-Publication Data

ISBN: 978-1-4985-9916-0 (cloth)
ISBN: 978-1-4985-9918-4 (pbk)
ISBN: 978-1-4985-9917-7 (electronic)

Contents

Acknowledgments

Cuba:

La Fundación Antonio Núñez Jiménez de la Naturaleza y el Hombre
La Unión de Escritores y Artistas de Cuba (UNEAC)
Universidad de la Habana

United States:

School of Marine and Atmospheric Sciences and Sustainability Studies Program, Stony Brook University
English Department, University of Idaho
University of Utah
Creative Writing Department, University of Arizona

Credits

Chapter 1: "Dimension Ambiental en Dos Textos de Excilia Saldaña." *La Gaceta de Cuba* vol. 1 (2017).

Chapter 3: "Hombres y mujeres de la tierra en los textos de viaje martianos." *ILE, Anuario de Ecologia, Cultura y Sociedad.* No. 3.3 (2003).

Chapter 5: Margarita Mateo Palmer, "Lydia Cabrera and The Narrative of Nature," REVOLUCIÓN Y CULTURA.

Chapter 6: "The New World Baroque as Postcolonial Ecology in Alejo Carpentier's The Lost Steps." This essay was originally published in *Postcolonial Ecologies* (Oxford UP 2011), George B. Handley.

Chapter 7: "Cuban Theatre and the Dilemma of Nature." *ISLE: Interdisciplinary Studies in Literature and Environment* 22.4 (Autumn 2015).

Chapter 11: "Siguiendo a Kengue." *La Gaceta de Cuba* vol. 1 (2017).

Chapter 12: Robert Michael Pyle, "The Cuba Poems," *Rain Magazine* © 2017.

Chapter 13: "Restauración." *La Gaceta de Cuba* vol. 1 (2017).

Chapter 14: "Poesia puertorriqueña y sueños de indepencia." *La Gaceta de Cuba* vol. 1 (2017).

Chapter 15: "El trompo: en la Sierra Maestra con la Guerilla de Teatreros." *La Gaceta de Cuba* vol. 1 (2017).

Introduction

Scott Slovic and David Taylor

Ernest Hemingway's posthumous novel *Islands in the Stream* (1970) details the life of a character named Thomas Hudson, who moved from the U.S. mainland to the Bimini Islands fifty miles east of Miami in pursuit of maritime adventure, a laid-back life among the local people of African descent, and the daily pleasure of island breezes. Some three hundred miles southwest of Bimini, two hundred miles from Miami, is Havana, Cuba, where Hemingway actually lived intermittently between 1939 and 1960, creating a homestead called Finca Vigia ("lookout farm") on the edge of town. The island in the Gulf Stream that Hemingway actually knew best, and where he helped create a Caribbean mythology that has tantilized the imagination of North Americans for more than half a century, is Cuba. Despite the ominous undertones of WWII U-boats (and sharks) passing through the Caribbean waters in *Islands in the Stream*, the book also portrays an island pastoralism where the protagonist awakens to "a light breeze blowing and out across the flats the sand was bone white under the blue sky and the small high clouds that were traveling with the wind made dark moving patches on the green water" (53–54). Today's visitor to Havana, or city resident, is more likely to experience the sea as a choppy body of dark water where few boats, aside from foreign cruise ships, are allowed. Most people in Cuba's capital city experience the Havana Harbor by walking along the Malecón, a five-mile esplanade along the seawall, looking down upon the rocky shoreline. The gap between Hemingway's Caribbean imaginary and the reality of contemporary urban experience in Cuba is palpable.

But just as Hemingway's portrayal of the Caribbean in the 1940s is a far stretch from certain aspects of today's reality, so too does Havana represent only a small facet of Cuban environmental culture. American environmentalists have long looked at modern Cuba as a model of progressive environmental thinking. Since the 1980s, Cuba has successfully tackled such problems as deforestation and garbage dumps resulting from poverty through vigorous restoration efforts. Cuba is known as the location of the Caribbean's largest protected wetland, the Cienaga de Zapata Biosphere Reserve. Rachel Cernansky argued in her 2012 article "Why Cuba's Sustainability Is Not an Accident" that some of Cuba's sustainable practices have been "framed as accidental choices" because "embargo restrictions have made it difficult to get things like pesticides and traditional building materials," but "the government deserves credit for integrating sustainability, very intentionally, into policy initiatives." As Fidel Castro stated in his 1992 speech at the Earth Summit in Rio de Janeiro, "Between 1992 and 1998, the National Assembly of People's Power amended the Cuban constitution to entrench the concept of sustainable development; the National Environment and Development Program was developed . . . ; an overarching environment law was passed; and a natoinal environment strategy was launched" (Cernansky). Daniel Whittle and Orlando Rey Santos, in "Protecting Cuba's Environment" (2006), highlight the specific role of Cuba's Ministry of Science, Technology, and Environment (CITMA), which founded in 1994, in safeguarding "the ecological crown jewel of the Caribbean, with more than 3,000 miles of coastline, spectacular coral reefs, massive mangrove wetlands, tropical wet forests, coastal mountains, caves, and rich biodiversity unmatched in the region" (74).

At the same time North American scholars of environmental policy, such as Whittle and Santos, were beginning to detail the trend-setting actions of the Cuban regime, specialists in the environmental humanities were also turning their attention to the Caribbean region. Elizabeth M. DeLoughrey, Renée K. Gosson, and George B. Handley helped to launch the now-burgeoning subdiscipline of postcolonial ecocriticism with their 2005 collection *Caribbean Literature and the Environment: Between Nature and Culture*, which builds upon the premise of Martinican cultural theorist Édouard Glissant's statement that the Caribbean "landscape is its own monument: its meaning can only be traced on the underside. It is all history" (*Caribbean Literature*, 1). The 2005 volume helped to revolutionize ecocritical practice by placing the efforts of the environmental justice movement into an international context, recognizing the inextricability of social justice (indeed, of *all* human action) and the physical world of nature. The specific impetus for *Caribbean Lierature and the Environment* was to "create a dialogue between the growing field of environmental literary studies, which has been primarily concerned with white settler narratives, and Caribbean cultural production, especially the region's negotiation of complex ethnic legacies" (2). The editors note in their introduction that the dialectical relationship between the region's violent colonial history and its verdant natural history "presents particular poetic and environmental opportunities" (3). Perhaps the earliest gesture to recognize the significant literary engagement with the Caribbean environment is Seodial Deena's essay "The Caribbean: Colonial and Postcolonial Representations of the Land and the People's Relationship to Their Environment," which appeared in Patrick D. Murphy's *Literature of Nature: An International Sourcebook* (1998).

More than a decade after DeLoughrey, Gosson, Handley, and the contributors to their volume helped to launch the scholarly movement that has become known as postcolonial ecocriticism (or "poco ecocrit"), it is difficult to say that ecocriticism continues to focus its attention on "white settler narratives." The discipline has become wonderfully diverse, producing a raft of green postcolonial monographs and collections, from Graham Huggan and Helen Tiffin's *Postcolonial Ecocriticism: Literature, Animals, Environment* (2010) to Rob Nixon's *Slow Violence and the Environmentalism of the Poor* (2011). At the same time, there has been a growing movement of environmental scholarship focusing on Hispanic literature and culture, including such books as Adrian Taylor Kane's *The Natural World in Latin American Literaures: Ecocritical Essays* (2010), Laura Barbas-Rhoden's *Ecological Imaginations in Latin American Fiction* (2012), and the collection *Ecological Crisis and Cultural Representation in Latin America: Ecocritical Perspectives on Art, Film, and Literature* (2016), edited by Mark Anderson and Zélia M. Bora. Whereas earlier ecocritical approaches to Latin American culture, tend to treat specific national or regional cultures (Amazonia, the Caribbean, the Southern Cone) in a semi-isolated fashion, the thrust in the later volume prepared by Anderson and Bora, is toward viewing Latin America in a global context. Anderson writes in his "Introduction: The Dimensions of Crisis":

> Objectively, there is undeniably an environmental crisis occurring on a planetary scale that has manifested itself in Latin America in unprecedented habitat loss, deforestation, species extinctions, land cover change due to the expansion of industrialized monoculture and mineral and hydrocarbon extraction, erosion, melting glaciers, environmental toxicity, and pollution in cities. . . . As natural as it may seem, much of the landscape we know as Latin America today is actually the result of catastrophic land cover changes wrought through the dispossession and genocide of millions of indigenous people and the implementation on a massive scale of extractive colonial land management practices such as large-scale mining, sugarcane monoculture, and cattle ranching. The majority of the cultures that are viewed as "traditionally" Latin American have historically been deeply embedded in these activities. (x)

For the most part, though, Cuba has been excluded from the examination of environmental cultural production and environmental crisis in volumes of humanitics research. One prominent exception is Reinaldo Funes Monzote's *From Rainforest to Cane Field in Cuba: An Environmental History since 1492* (*Envi-*

sioning Cuba), which is the definitive environmental history of Cuba. The lone Cuba-focused study in *Caribbean Literature and the Environment* is Antonio Benitez-Rojo's "Sugar and the Environment in Cuba," while only the final article in *Ecological Crisis and Cultural Representations in Latin America*, Marcela Reales Visbal's "Tourism, Ecology, and Changing US-Cuban Relations," zeroes in on Cuba in the 2016 collection—and this particular international relationship is in flux as we prepare the current volume.

Even as ecocritics from North America have turned their attention to the colonial and postcolonial histories of agricultural development and touristic exploitation (and appreciation) on the island of Cuba, there has persisted an American fascination with Cuban natural history. David Gessner exemplifies the latter in his 2007 book *Soaring with Fidel: An Osprey Odyssey from Cape Cod to Cuba and Beyond*, in which he follows migrating birds from New England to the Caribbean, ultimately visiting La Gran Piedra on the southeastern shore near Santiago de Cuba, where, he writes, "There may be better places to watch birds, but there are none more spectacular" (170). Of the third-largest stone monolith in the world, Gessner notes:

> To get to the stairs and the path that led up to the rock I had to slip through the bar of the town's one hotel and pay the bartender a dollar, but once I started climbing, the rainforest closed in, water dripping from plants and bugs buzzing. Farther up the steps I passed a black pig rooting in the ferns right off the trail. The red mud was slippery and puddles covered the steps, and my heart pounded from both the climb and the excitement. . . . Four hundred and fifty steps later I reached the side of La Gran Piedra itself, a huge hunk of volcanic rock. . . . I emerged from a kind of tunnel through the rainforest to find a ladder bolted into its side. The ladder led straight up, and when I reached the top, I felt dizzy and exhilarated. I'd stood on the top of plenty of mountains in my life, but the rock had a kind of booster effect, as if it were a small mountain on top of another mountain. . . . The view *was* boundless. (171)

The current volume is a hybrid collection of ecocritical and literary responses to the Cuban environment and to Cuban environmental culture. DeLoughrey, Gosson, and Handley refer to the "complex ethnic legacies" of the region, implying the mestizaje cultural blend of Ibero-European, Afro-Caribbean, and North American skin tones, voices, musical predilections, cuisines, agricultural practices, and so on. To these, *An Island in the Stream* adds the convergences and shared conversations between humanities scholars and literary artists and between American and Cubans during the second decade of the twenty-first century. While we do not claim that *An Island in the Stream* is a full-scale study of Cuban environmental policy and activism, or even an encyclopedic survey of Cuban environmental culture, it does represent a new foray on the part of environmental humanities scholars and artists from both the United States and Cuba to engage in a dialogue that we hope will bear fruit in future collaborations and educational exchanges.

The seed for this book is the project led by Melinda Levin and David Taylor to bring together students and faculty members from the University of North Texas to meet with Cuban professors, city historians, scientists, sustainability experts, and artists in order to "better understand Cuba's unique situation in sustainability in the Western hemisphere," as Taylor and Levin put it in their introduction to a special cluster of articles and poems that appeared in the Autumn 2015 issue of *ISLE: Interdisciplinary Studies in Literature and Environment* until the title "Artes y Medio Ambiente Realización (Performing Arts and the Environment): Cuban Theatre Performances about the Environment." The students and faculty from Texas began visiting Cuba in May 2014, and in addition to meeting with sustainabillty experts, they quickly found themselves engaged with the vibrant Cuban cultural scene, including music, literature, and the visual and performing arts. By the time the Cuban work had been published in *ISLE*, Taylor had moved to join the faculty at Stony Brook University in New York, where he continued to bring students with him to experience the lifestyles and landscapes of Cuba. It also occurred to him that it might be possible to accelerate collaborations between American and Cuban environmental writers and scholars if he organized a symposium on literature and environment. After months of planning, the Encuentro Literature y Medio Ambiente, hosted by Liliana Núñez and Armando Fernandez, took place on December 7–8, 2016, at the Fundacion Antonio Nuñez Jiménez de la Naturaleza y el Hombre in Havana with approximately twenty participants. Americans Alison Hawthorne Deming, Blas Falconer, Wendy Harding, Robert Michael Pyle, Scott Slovic, and Sylvia Torti joined Taylor and their Cuban counterparts, including Mayra Beatriz Martinez and Mariana Serra García, in offering short readings and lectures. Dozens of black-and-white photographs of Fidel Castro, who had died a week before the Americans arrived in Havana for the symposium, graced the bookshelves of the reading room where the presentations took place, providing a suitable background. For the purposes of this collection, we are pleased to include articles by Gabriel Horowitz, Susan Bender, Margarita Mateo Palmer, George B. Handley, Karina Pino Gallardo, Christina Maria Garcia, and Heriberto Feraudy Espino in addition to work by participants in the December 2016 gathering.

The scholarly approaches to Cuban environmental culture begin with Mariana Serra García considering the "environmental dimensions" of the work of recent Cuban author Excilia Saldaña (1946–1999), who was a poet, storyteller, essayist, editor, translator, journalist, and professor. In Saldaña's writings, Serra García discerns the cultural hybridity that postcolonial scholars, including ecocritics, have determined to be one of the abiding characteristics of Caribbean culture. Serra García focuses, in particular, on the West

African rituals and terms that have made their way into Cuba's "mixed ethno-culture." Gabriel Horowitz takes readers on a historical survey of representations of Niagara Falls by three Cuban authors—José Martí, Juan A. Pérez Bonalde, and José María Heredia—and reading in their work varying degrees of using natural description to create "a fantasy of nature—of a place that stands outside of the flow of history, but which reinforces its repetition through the erasure of history." Horowitz's consideration of Cuban literary representations of North America provides a fitting counterpart to other works in this collection, such as Alison Deming's poem, that emphasize North American views of Cuba. Mayra Beatriz Martinez's next focuses her study of the travel writings of iconic Cuban author José Martí (1853–1895), particularly his representations of nature in such publications as "Mother America," "Our America," and *Manifesto of Montecristi*, which discerns in Martí's work a tendency to promote Caribbean stereotypes of nature and people.

The mixing of cultures emphasized in Mariana Serra García's article is also a theme in Susan Bender's portrait of polyglot Cuban adventurer Antonio Nuñez Jiménez (1923–1998) and Ecuadorian painter and sculptor Oswaldo Guayasamín (1919–1999), both of whom were supporters of Fidel Castro and the communist Cuban Revolution. While Nuñez Jiménez was particularly well known for his Humboldtian knowledge of Latin American and Caribbean natural history and anthropology, he did not develop his expertise in a vacuum, instead benefitting from the cultural ferment of pre- and postrevolutionary Cuba, including his friendship with artists such as Guayasamín. Margarita Mateo Palmer extends the approach taken in Mariana Serra García's article, focusing in this case on *Black Stories of Cuba* and *The Mountain* by Lydia Cabrera, which reveal the central concepts of Santeria, the Afro-Cuban religion, such as the spiritual meaning of mountains and the animate qualities of natural forces. In George B. Handley's study of Alejo Carpentier's *The Lost Steps*, reprinted in this volume, the focus is on the idea of "the primitive" in Carpentier's well-known novel, where indigenous human characters, conflated with wild jungle, implicitly give voice to nature itself. While some might criticize the apparent anthropocentrism of Carpentier's narrative, a biocentric reading helps to rehabilitate "the sense of ecology that is a kind of decentered humanism" in the novel.

Karina Pino Gallardo shifts our attention from the written text to the context of environmental performance by discussing "the landscape of the Cuban theater scene," tracing the field from the founding of the community-based Escambray Theater in the 1970s to the contemporary work of Jose Oriol González's Teatro de los Elementos, which extends the community-oriented focus to a theatrical practice "which is not abusive to the local landscape and is interested in dealing with any public environmental problems, whether it is pollution or the drying of a river." Christina Maria Garcia brings together the fictional imaginings of Havana's topography in Antonio José Ponte's 2007 novel *La fiesta vigilada* with a 2009 sculptural installation in Havana by Roberto Fabelo, which augments the city's ubiquitous images of revolutionary heroes like Camilo Cienfuegos and Che Guevara with giant bronze cockroaches bearing human heads. To many outsiders, contemporary Cuban culture may seem shallowly nationalistic and uncritical, but Garcia's study provides a useful tonic in identifying "the waste left behind by the incessant drive towards a future and the desire to cultivate 'a scientific education necessary for the domination of available resources.'" Her ecocritical reading of *La fiesta vigilada* highlights the novel's subtle critique of revolutionary optimism, the foregrounding of dismal corporeality, and other tropes.

Following Garcia's pronouncement that Ponte "calls attention to our material and territorial interdependence, implying the interdependence of human communities and humans and other organisms (such as Fabelo's roaches), we offer a rich Appendix of "literary responses" to Cuban environmental culture. Many of the American delegates to the December 2016 symposium in Havana, even those who are better known as environmental humanities scholars, were inspired by the experience to write creative pieces in response to our visit to Cuba. We include this work here, as a gesture toward the interdependence between humanities scholarship and artistic expression, with the goal of cultural and environmental mindfulness and sensitivity. Heriberto Feraudy Espino contributes a retelling of a morality tale from Afro-Cuban mythology that explains what happens when human beings do not offer proper gratitude and care for the life-giving waters of their home places. Alison Hawthorne Deming's poem, "The Gardener's Creed," riffs hopefully on the experience of our delegation's week in Havana—"I believe the garden / can sew up wounds in a city," she writes. "Words too though words can open wounds anew." Indeed, one has the sense, strolling through the rubble of La Habana Vieja and inspecting the verdant campus of La Universidad de La Habana, that if we people were to vanish for a few weeks, or even a few hours, the 3,500 plants native to Cuba would somehow burst out of the Jardín Botánico Nacional and populate the brighly painted rubble with white ginger and La Mariposa—the Butterfly Flower (the national flower of Cuba)—and with actual butterflies.

In recounting her own perspective on the 2016 visit to Havana, biologist and author Sylvia Torti meditates on a thank you offered by our host Armando Fernandez to his American visitors—and to the United States more generally: "We thank the Americans for the embargo because it saved us from the perversion of commodities." By stepping out of her own culture in North America, a culture of physical and spiritual gluttony, Torti comes to understand that what she most desires "is the real and fulfilling sustenance of our individual and communal lives." Such sustenance—the sustenance of empanadas and old cars, of fisherman casting out and boys pulling in sea-perch, of soft-voiced children and polychromatic cats, of bats and tour guides and butterflies—is what literary lepidopterist Robert Michael Pyle supplies in a series of poetic anecdotes. Laura Ruíz Montes, too, highlights the restorative theme of Cuba in her poem, the repair of old appliances rather than the accumulation, the endless accumulation of new commodities—a strange alchemy of reuse enables "broken down things" in Cuba to appear "fragrant and fresh / as if nothing had ever happened there before." American poet Blas Falconer, of Puerto Rican descent, finds himself thinking of his island grandmother and of Laura Ruíz Montes's poem "Restauración" (included in this book), in crafting his own poem of longing and identity. "I'll wait beside you," he writes, "though / I don't know what we're waiting for." This is a sentiment that reverberated through many of the formal and informal statements of participants in the 2016 meeting, both Cuban and American. We wanted to be together, to interact, to share and receive, even if many of us did not know exactly what we expected to come from this convocation.

Perhaps David Taylor, more than the rest of us, knew what to expect from our gathering in Havana, having been to Cuba a number of times before, leading delegations of students and colleagues. His essay for this volume tells the story of touring the Cuban countryside with Guerilla de Teatreros, one of the country's community-nurturing theater organizations. Taylor was given a child's spinning toy, a top, during his visit, and he keeps this *trompo* on his office desk in New York to remind him today that we are all, regardless of where we live in the world, "riding a great *trompo* spinning, wobbling, possibly falling out of control." However, he concludes, "Perhaps in sharing our stories and our awareness of the need to care for our places and our planet, we begin to see we share so much." Scott Slovic concludes the book with his essay "Something Wonderful and Surreal," about the uncertain objectives and outcomes of the Cuban-American collaboration. He places the 2016 symposium—and, by extension, this book—in the context of various other convergences of international colleagues, in India and China and elsewhere, who take solace and gain strength from the humor, idealism, and insights shared at such meetings. "We were not alone," he writes. So ends this book—and perhaps, in a sense, this is the message of the environmental humanities.

WORKS CITED

Anderson, Mark. "Introduction: The Dimensions of Crisis." In *Ecological Crisis and Cultural Representation in Latin America: Ecocritical Perspectives on Art, Film, and Literature*, edited by Mark Anderson and Zélia M. Bora, pp. ix–xxxi. Lexington Books, 2016.

Anderson, Mark, and Zélia M. Bora, eds. *Ecological Crisis and Cultural Representation in Latin America: Ecocritical Perspectives on Art, Film, and Literature*. Lexington Books, 2016.

Barbas-Rhoden, Laura. *Ecological Imaginations in Latin American Fiction*. University Press of Florida, 2012.

Benítez-Rojo, Antonio. "Sugar and the Environment in Cuba." In *Caribbean Literature and the Environment: Between Nature and Culture*, edited by Elizabeth M. DeLoughrey, Renée K. Gosson, and George B. Handley, pp. 33–50. University of Virginia Press, 2005.

Cernansky, Rachel. "Why Cuba's Sustainability Is Not an Accident." *Treehugger* (April 20, 2012). https://www.treehugger.com/environmental-policy/why-cuba-sustainability-not-accident.html

Deena, Seodial. "The Caribbean: Colonial and Postcolonial Representations of the Land and the People's Relationship to Their Environment." In *Literature of Nature: An International Sourcebook*, edited by Patrick D. Murphy, pp. 366–73. Fitzroy Dearborn Publishers, 1998.

DeLoughrey, Elizabeth M., Renée K. Gosson, and George B. Handley, eds. *Caribbean Literature and the Environment: Between Nature and Culture*. University of Virginia Press, 2005.

Funes Monzote, Reinaldo. *From Rainforest to Cane Field in Cuba: An Environmental History since 1492 (Envisioning Cuba)*. University of North Carolina Press, 2008.

Gessner, David. *Soaring with Fidel: An Osprey Odyssey from Cape Cod to Cuba and Beyond*. Beacon, 2007.

Hemingway, Ernest. *Islands in the Stream*. Scribner, 1970.

Huggan, Graham, and Helen Tiffin. *Postcolonial Ecocriticism: Literature, Animals, Environment*. Routledge, 1010.

Kane, Adrian Taylor. *The Natural World in Latin American Literatures: Ecocritical Essays on Twentieth Century Writings*. McFarland, 2010.

Nixon, Rob. *Slow Violence and the Environmentalism of the Poor*. Harvard University Press, 2011.

Taylor, David, and Melinda Levin, coord. "Artes y Medio Ambiente Realización (Performing Arts and the Environment): Cuban Theatre Performances about the Enviornment." *ISLE: Interdisciplinary Studies in Literature and the Environment* 22.4 (Autumn 2015): 873–900.

Visbal, Marcela Reales. "Tourism, Ecology, and Changing US-Cuban Relations." In *Ecological Crisis and Cultural Representation in Latin America: Ecocritical Perspectives on Art, Film, and Literature*, edited by Mark Anderson and Zélia M. Bora, pp. 277–90. Lexington Books, 2016.

Whittle, Daniel, and Orlando Rey Santos. "Protecting Cuba's Environment: Efforts to Design and Implement Effective Environmental Laws and Policies in Cuba." *Cuban Studies* 37 (2006): 73–103.

Chapter One

Environmental Dimensions in Two of Excilia Saldaña's Texts

Mariana G. Serra García,
Translated by Joy Dinkelman

Excilia Saldaña (1946–1999)—poet, storyteller, essayist, editor, translator, journalist, and professor—started to publish her books for children and adolescents during the last quarter of the past century. Her fascinating and transgressive work—compared by one scholar to a raging hurricane (González)—has resisted classification. This chapter will apply ecofeminist discourse to characterize key aspects of two of Saldaña's works.

An important feature of her work is constructed when, in the context of Western culture, she looks to recover a goddess from a prepatriarchal myth as an alternative to the masculine predominance of God.[1] In this way, she seeks to reestablish equilibrium between us and our world (Leeming and Page, 4). The myth of Gaia, the Greek Mother Earth, is particularly prominent in popular and scientific imagery. Gaia's paradoxical conduct in the thirtieth part of the *Homeric Hymns* is at times benevolent and at other times merciless, much as James Lovelock has represented in developing his Gaia hypothesis. For Lovelock, Gaia has the capacity to autoregulate and to unconsciously preserve the planet as it was adapted for life; if humanity continues on its actual path, it will be eliminated as punishment for its anthropocentric excesses (Lovelock, 228).

Saldaña's ecofeminist discourse is a prominent aspect of her award-winning book, *Songs for a Mayito and a Dove* (1983).[2] The title points to a communion between human beings and nonhumans. The author also dedicated the book to David, her own bird, who is described as "the owner of the river and of the treasured mystery." The unconventional opening to the book is a presentation of a mythic being, the Deaf Weaver of the River (also described as the "Ring of the Weavers"). The book deals with Oshún, an Orisha (a minor god) of the Osha Rule or Cuban Santeria. The stories told in this work have not been separated from the Yoruba African religion, but are the result of a syncretic process, with its appropriations, losses, and transmutations of Yoruba myths to a socially and ecologically different environment. In Africa, there is river named after Oshún. But in Cuba, Oshún becomes the generic river, with the connotation of the unstoppable progress of life: "From its riverbed time, she separates herself from the story of the river" (Rodríguez). Oshún is a goddess who has many ups and downs or paths and attributes; her dominions are fertility, beauty, love, and sensuality. In Saldaña's texts, besides being "deaf," Oshún lacks omnipotence: "individual mothers trust in the weaver's hands to protect them. But a single pair of hands cannot do all the things that, together, all the hands can do" (Saldaña, 7).

Saldaña's writing simulates the possession rite of the Orisha. "Habitat" or "home" in the Yoruba tongue is *ilé*; this in key concept in Yoruba religion. Saldaña's Oshún works miracles with a pumpkin, transforming it into a kind of habitat—she lives in it. The narrator says: "I lived in a pumpkin inside of a pumpkin patch" (Saldaña, 13). "Pumpkin patch" refers not only to a pumpkin plant, but also to a village near Havana, but what is referred to by the narrator is neither the people nor the city: "it was all the sites and something more" (Saldaña, 13). In the utopic space described in the story, both the mythic pumpkin patch and the actual Cuban environment and social context are implied. If Oshún is the mother of the Cuban nation, then the voices of the text are trying to recompose the nation's historical-cultural narrative.

Saldaña's story begins with the poems "First Lesson" and "Cane," not as religious hymns, but as songs seeking to describe a jointly developed identity of nature and a peculiar cultural history. Nature is represented here by "the form and behavior of wood-warblers, hummingbirds and sparrows and other living beings" (Saldaña, 31). These animals are the first teachers. The other great teacher is a grandmother, the master of the house ("jute skirt [sign of Babalú], striped shirt, white apron"), of course a Mulatta ("Manila shawl, wrap bracelets and coral earrings," also *daughter* of Oshún) (Saldaña, 23). The grandmother represents the oral transmission of traditional culture; she tells the stories and introduces the mysteries of life as a kind of *witchdoctor* because she knows the secrets of ointments prepared with herbs and animal fat. The granddaughter in Saldaña's story dreamed about being the farmer of the stars; she dreamed of plowing the earth and sowing the dawn, of being the dew drops, rain, and rainbow, and of being the island trees for the *mayitos* and the doves. She made her dream of farming the stars come true, as the child of Mr. Sky and Mrs. Sea. For her—and for the other children in the story—such phrases as "Ovillejo for the son" and "Nana for the doves to sleep" describe what was given to them by the gods (Saldaña, 23).

The two following sections of Saldaña's book point to the work of Nicolas Guillén and his expression of our own mixed ethnoculture. One of his core ideas is the representation of the grandmother of the African lineage in Cuban culture; specifically, Guillén refers to Ma Teodora, or Teodora Ginés (1530–1598), a freed slave and Dominican musician who is considered the composer of the song "Son de la Má Teodora" around the year 1562, which symbolizes the foundation of Cuban culture. Saldaña's grandmother character tells her story in the mode of fantasy, using the borrowed clothing of popular Spanish hymnbooks: "The owner of all crossroads" (Elegguá—one of the most important orishas in Santeria), "one-footed Osaín," "The bottom of the sea" (where only Olokun can live), and "Osará, the wind" (in the hope that it refreshes the dreams of her son) (Saldaña, 54). "Nana of the slave" indicates the presence of Our Lady of Mercy, the other grandmother, who has eyes full of pain because despite her white skin she is neither free nor happy. Equally generous, she sows and cares for plants, opens the birdcage, and calms an orphan with warm milk. Both are evoked by emotional memories, especially by the smell and the taste of her homemade sweets. Other meanings of the hybridized biological and cultural heritage are seen in such phrases as "Riddles of the Guitarist," "Round," and "My Mother of Pearl Child" (Saldaña, 57).

Next to the legend of the gods, the grandmothers also remember the legendary times of the liberation and the brotherhood of all Cubans. Therefore, the grandmothers sing to the most excellent and everlasting heroes, Ovillejo of Maceo and Martí. With these same grandmothers, we learn to drink Cuba Libre, not the well-known rum with Coke, but the combination of honey, water, and lime, as well as to love *Cuba Libre* (Free Cuba). Together these drinks celebrate the fact that, with the assault on the Moncada, the future arrives in which their island does not look like a sleeping or defeated caiman, but instead stands proud. Singing a final song to the "Revolution," the narration concludes: "there was a feast there in my pumpkin patch . . . the feast that will never end. My feast is also your feast, the feast that your children will also celebrate" (Saldaña, 79). Therefore, in effect, the Deaf Weaver of the River has gone on weaving dreams, realizations, stories, proclamations, guesses, lullabies, myths and histories, personal and collective memories, and nature and culture, "to create the tapestry of Cuban nationality" (Rodriguez).

Certainly, in *Kele Kele* (1987), Saldaña accomplishes a true feminist manuscript, although she did not restrict herself to the legends of Obba and Oyá (Vadillo). She starts the book with the three children. They are Olofi's daughters, raised in the same manner, with the same kindness and beauty, in love with the same man: Orula appeals to the father to cure them of the evils of love. Orula speaks through Ifa, who recommended that they work on an antidote. With a clear purpose, they make the girls leave their parents' home in search of their destiny. The first two are defeated by Ikú (death), skilled in camouflage, with the poison of his lies. The third, at the request of her father, gets together provisions "of honey, eggs, egg fruit and five pieces of sweet bread, two different kinds of colored sugars, cinnamon sticks and powdered cinnamon, and anise in the form of a star for hunger; for thirst, an *igbá* full of fresh water; for the nights, a click beetle and a firefly" (Saldaña, 79). With all those things, she rides a log raft and hurls herself downriver, in search of her sisters. In this way the story represents one of the paths of Oshún and her election to be the woman and secretary of Orula. As the third daughter travels by river, the current is soft and sweet; apparently the river and orisha are the same thing. The daughter is not frightened before Ikú, nor does she accept an agreement with him, because neither honor, nor freedom, nor love have a price to her. Her body suffers from the rigor of her travel across the earth. She looks at everything that surrounds her (both natural and man-made landscapes), but she is sure that "only the one who arrives triumphs, and only one who perseveres arrives" (Saldaña, 79). This is the secret that is revealed by this orisha, without which she would be punished like the princess Sikán from the Abakan myth. The fundamentals of its strength—the heart, trust, love, and courage—are venerated with the expression *Ma fe re fun*, because they make it possible to turn fantasy into reality. A white space in the text graphically accentuates the idea of distance with a demystifying feeling. Later, married to Orula-Ifá-Orunmila, the third daughter repeats the words: "We will build a future upon the ruins of the past" (Saldaña, 40–41). This is another violation of custom, because as a woman she is forbidden to repeat or interpret the voice of Ifá. Only the male priests of Ifá have that authority. He, like the grandmother, speaks with the wise refrain: "Underneath the sun nothing is easy, the rope always gets tangled" (Saldaña, 40–41). The narrator's voice says: "Thus ends the story that I came to tell you today; yesterday my grandmother told me, tomorrow you will repeat it" (Saldaña, 40–41). This story has a happy ending—the sincerity of love and the mutual respect that unite a couple.

A poem about the animism of nature acts as a hinge between the preceding story and *La lechuza y el sijú* (*The Witch Owl and the Sijú* [a nocturnal bird native to Cuba]); this story demonstrates that love at first sight can be eternal. Again, there is ambivalence: a surreal space for fantastic things to occur that at the same time refers to the actual revolutionary Cuban in the reader, where "only the children and adolescents will be able to be princes and princesses" (Saldaña, 51). The primary character in the story loves everything that surrounds her because everything is what she is, and one day this feeling awakens a wanderer who arrives on the path of surprises. Annoyed, she talks to an old woman (a reoccurrence of the grandmother character), who advises her to consult exterior nature (listen for three days to the hummingbirds and the canary, respectively) and her inner feelings. She recommends the same to the wanderer, in order to extinguish the fire/desire that devours him. The two project an eternal and complementary union: he is thunder and she is lightning (Changó and Oyá); he enters the hill and she lures him out with honey (Oggún and Oshún); the sea and sand; the earth and rain; the tree and nest. One day, he shall walk up and say to her: "Now your purpose is to tell your people the story of my people. Tell it to them. Weave your baskets and fill them with butterflies and click beetles. And wait for me. Wait for me, so we will make the future a party" (Saldaña, 51). But the story does not end like Penelope and Odysseus because "on the Tree of Eternal Truths—another tree, for the liars, is nothing different—the princess, transformed into the *Lechuza* (Witch Owl), watches over the night, and *Sijú*, her lover, whistles to her to tell her that he's already back" (Saldaña, 51).

Neither one of the two following stories has a happy ending, like the poem that precedes Obba's poem[3] suggests: "When love is torn, you cannot reclose the banks" (Saldaña, 56). The two phrases repeated from the beginning are leit motifs: "How beautiful she was! How pretty and black she was!" which implies a discrepancy with the imposition of Western stereotypes about the beauty of the female body (Saldaña, 56). Born "of only one dream, only one desire and only one promise" (Saldaña, 56), well brought up and very hardworking (especially in the kitchen), the protagonist has similar qualities to the princesses of classical tales, but is the opposite of Snow White and especially her evil stepmother, who consults the magic mirror about her beauty and future. The black princess confronts Orula and his *ekuelé*. Ifá says that everyone has a decided future: "What Olofi writes at night, man cannot erase during the day" (Saldaña, 56). She recognized herself with pride as Obbalube, "born to be that" (Saldaña, 59). This name alludes to the syncretism of the orishas (*Reglas de Osha* and *Palo Monte*). In order to give them something to eat in times of war and hunger, Obba prepared a favorite dish, *amalá* (flour with okra), and would add meat from her own ears. At the discovery of the mutilation, Changó disowned her as a woman, although he maintained her as his wife. This version of the traditional story accentuates an extraliterary concern, the idea of questionable social conduct: in a culture of machismo, the "perfect" housewife, because of her submissiveness, lost the respect of her husband and others. Condemned to cry about her pain in solitude, the princess's tears form a river: "to which go the abandoned women to drown in the current of their horrible memories. Only the bad memories" (Saldaña, 63).

Between this story and that of Oyá, re-created in their contrasting behavior, a poem is inserted that, in the style of an *oru*, invokes "the kings of the lightning and thunder" to wipe out centuries of social injustice and racial discrimination (Saldaña, 92). Later, Oyá interrupts "with his tunic made of wind," "to sprinkle in our faces an old, old tale"; his voice is whispering, like when he was young and still playing "with Butterfly Needle, good herbs, butterflies, and lilies," very softly (*kele kele*), "as if repeating to oneself the secret of some myth" (Saldaña, 92). Feeling predestined "to convert all the earth into an orchard," requesting the training of a *petedbisa*, because, "besides helping her husband with *kofá* issues, she is a good seamstress" (Saldaña, 92), the young woman longs to be a dream weaver too. The story outlines the characters, and the young woman's own voice weaves in and out of the narrative flow. It defines the time: "skillful seller of some rare medicine that turns people grey and shortens their lifespan" (Saldaña, 92). Their passing is marked by the eternal cycle of the seasons. With the spring, Oyá releases "the cane shaft, the needles, and the wheel" (Saldaña, 92). In summer, she remains forever enthralled by Changó, so she rejects the rest of her suitors. She desires a relationship on equal footing, based on love. Oggún appears—the hunter, owner of the hills and iron, warrior of great excellence. The same thing happens to him that happened to Oyá with respect to Changó; they never have the heart of their loved one. When the rumbling drums announce Changó and Obba's wedding, the madness of Oyá turns into a ruthless hurricane. Meanwhile a lyrical lament is sung. Oyá becomes the lady of lightning, of maelstroms, of the rainbow, seated at the cemetery's gate. A fratricidal duel between Changó and Oggún is to the death. In Yansa's land, Oyá intervenes to save Changó with a trick: she disguises him with her clothes and her braids. It is a simulation of transvestitism because Changó is an androgynous deity, syncretically merged with Santa Barbara. It is said that the traditional ruler of Oyó was demoralized and became an orisha, symbolized by a terrible earthquake and a violent storm. His women are the river and sisters of Obba: Oyá and Oshún. Changó and Oyá are forever united by a strange agreement, not generated by love or loyalty, but by "the betrayal of that one night set against the Hill, against their Majesty" (Saldaña, 92).[4] Obviously, the antiracist feeling of this poetic invocation focuses in the symbolism of the story on the relationship of a human couple. However, the metaphor of treachery on the hill lends itself to an ecological reading; the treachery provokes a violent vengeance in the divine trinity and not only of the omnipotent goddess, as conceived in the metaphor of Gaia. The powerful capacity for protection and destruction is attributed to the three orisha without caring about the differences in sex. Oyá, in particular, is ambiguous: both a hurricane and a rainbow.

"Kele kele" closes the namesake book; it has as a brief opening inscription: "If you hear him say to the sun that he always dries everything he finds, then ask him if perhaps he knows what it is and where the river is" (Saldaña, 101). Biotic and abiotic beings of nature believe that they know their identities, but their true identities can only be revealed by those who control the stories: "The river is a woman and in the hill she submerges herself. Skin like the earth, the body an eternal seed, breath from a soft wind, laughs of happy birds and humid clouds in the gaze where there exists no death" (Saldaña,

101). This passage presents a metaphor of the eternal rebirth of life. New definitions of time are given accordingly: "there is no word for that which never was and yet is alive" (Saldaña, 101).

It is said that Olofi, in the form of a dove, calls for a solution to the environmental crisis that was created by Oggún, Oyá, and Changó. After pleading, with a song, to open the paths so that human beings and gods could go to a nonexistent country, where they will sit together under the shade of *iroko* (teak), they prepare *omiero* (herbal wash) and consult with the coconuts, while the little *Ibbeyis* (orishas) play. Later on, they start an assembly. Everyone participates, except the accused and Obba. Feisitá (one of the avatars and paths of Oshún) is the secretary. Olofi states that "we did not come to judge old, past actions; if Thunder is fair, the Hill is noble, [and] Squall is good. Every day comes by itself and alone it has to leave. We did not come to decide who the best is or who is worse, we came to save a brother that is on the verge of death" (Saldaña, 101). All the orishas (Yemayá, Obatalá, Eleggúa, Olokum, Babalú Ayé, one-footed Osaín, Orisha Oko, Obanlá, Agayú, and Inlé) agree with the locations of the pantheon. The passion and commotion grow. It irritates Babalú because it seems to him like they are in a *bembé* (an Afro-Cuban drum); he asks Olofi to regain order and declare that those who think that rules are golden obtain positions of power. Here is where the political and social context becomes clear.

The assembly is prolonged; everyone is tired, but they decide to continue on with it. Then Oshún arrives, and they propose to entrust her with the issue because she possesses the secret key of using discretion. She promises that every tree will once again stand up; the plants will flower, and the animals will return. She assures that the struggle is already over, *oñí* (honey) is already flowing through the hills, and that Oggún opened them so that it will never cease again.

An ecofeminist discussion of Saldaña's work does not give a clear image of the Gaian implications, but such an approach tends to demystify the orishas by emphasizing the dilemma of predestination versus the liberty to choose, favoring the idea of individual responsible action—of respecting one another—in ways that support the diversity of being. Likewise, the text does not accentuate gender differences in nature: the forces of nature are mixed, revealing both destructive and regenerative capacities, represented anthropomorphically to show both feminine and masculine features. Reestablishing ecological and social harmony requires the keys of inclusion, respect, and love. Saldaña's books, which are deliberately educational, point toward a cultural paradigm shift.

NOTES

1. Niall Binns—in his *Dead End? The Ecological Crisis in Latin American Poetry* (Zaragoza: University Press of Zaragoza, 2004), chapter 4, "The American Awakening of Gaia: Ecologism, Ecofeminism and Traditionalism in Gabriela Mistral," p. 93—considers the publication consistent with such studies as *Lost Goddesses of Early Greece* (1978) by Charlene Spretnak; *The Goddess: Mythological Images of the Feminine* (1981) by Christine Downing; *When God Was a Woman* (1976) by Merlin Stone; *The Goddesses in Every-woman* by Jean Shinoda (1984); *Eros and the Womanliness of God* (1986) by Ingrid Shafer; *The Reflowering of the Goddess* (1990) by Gloria F Orenstein; and *Goddess: Myths of the Female Divine* (1994) by David Leeming and Jake Page.

2. Received mention in The Age of Gold contest and the Ismaelillo children's literature award in the genre of poetry, in UNEAC, in 1979, and the Rosa Blanca Award in 1984.

3. Alicia E. Vadillo: "In another form of reading, the initial presence of poems can be understood as a contemporary «letter» from Ifá. This possible 'odu' or figure that opens the narrative text proceeding the destiny of the in love orisha. Now, the author moves the feminine appreciation to herself to attribute the right to interpret the divine prediction contained in the poem or 'letter.' With her action she breaks the limitations imposed on her sex by the Yoruban religious system by showing herself to be similar to a *babalawo* and, from this sacred position, interprets the actual voice of Orula" ("A Feminist Manuscript").

4. According to the interpretation of Alicia E. Vadillo: Oyá "promises to Changó her services of making the bed, services that are not related to being with him or being the best 'housewife' but with being his equal, his help in the battle against his eternal rival Oggún. . . . It is known that without the help of a female . . . Changó, as the original story says, was afraid of Oggún, and would not be the victor" ("A Feminist Manuscript," p. 92).

WORKS CITED

González, Flora M. *In the Vortex of the Cyclone*. Translated by Rosamond Rosenmeier and prefaced by Nancy Morejón. University Press of Florida, 2002.

Leeming, David, and Jake Page. *Goddess: Myths of the Female Divine*. Oxford University Press, 1994.

Lovelock, James. *Gaia, a New Vision of Life on Earth*. Orbis, 1985.

Rodríguez, Antonio Orlando. "Excilia Saldaña in Memoriam." Digital Review. *Cuatrogatos*. https://www.cuatrogatos.org/detail-articulos.php?id=114

Saldaña, Excilia. *Songs for a Mayito and a Dove (Cantos para un mayito y una paloma)*. New People Editorial, 2007.

Vadillo, Alicia. "A Feminist Manuscript for 'Obba' and 'Oyá.'" In the digital review *La Isla en Peso*.

Chapter Two

Renewing Niagara Falls, Burning the Archive in the Cuban Poetic Tradition

Gabriel Horowitz

The concept of nature reinforces a logic of supersession that contains a paradoxical desire to return to the past and at the same time to destroy it. It is in this way that nature can be seen as a defining structure of modernity. The operation of this structure, while normally covert, becomes visible in the relation struck up between three nature poems about Niagara Falls, written by three different Caribbean writers over the course of the nineteenth century, and the commentary that José Martí writes (and does not write) about them.

At the beginning of *Divergent Modernities* (2001), Julio Ramos introduces José Martí's prologue to Juan A. Pérez Bonalde's "Poema del Niágara" (1882) as a crucial work that "constitutes one of the first Latin American reflections on the problematic relation between literature and power" after the first wave of national independences in the nineteenth century (Ramos, xxxv). Furthermore, Ramos calls attention to the fact that the "crisis" that Martí addresses, an "*exhaustion* of traditional modes of literary representation," is "concomitant with what Max Weber termed the disenchantment of the world in the process of rationalization and secularization" (Ramos, xxxvii). For Ramos, the prologue is not only an expression of a crisis within Latin America, but is also symptomatic of a larger crisis of modernity akin to that described in depth by Theodor Adorno and Max Horkheimer in *Dialectic of Enlightenment.*[1]

Ramos uses the expression "exile from the polis" to describe Martí's characterization of modernity, making a symbol out of the Cuban writer's very real experience of exile in the United States. What Ramos goes on to describe casts this exile from the polis—a trope defined by the relation between the center and the periphery, city, and wilderness—as an unsettled positioning between the past and the present. He shows how on the one hand Martí feels the need to break with the burden of a tradition that can be understood also as a kind of *law*, the "paternal institution" (xxxviii). But on the other, he seeks to reaffirm this law and reclaim its legitimacy: "against the 'sugeon's scalpel,' an emblem for the official positivism of the epoch, Martí hearkens to the romantic impulses of a previous age, proposing the romantic priority of 'a knowledge bequeathed to me by the gaze of children'" (xxxix). By highlighting the difficulty of navigating a desire to break with the law of the father and a desire to reinscribe it, Ramos shows that Martí's exile from the polis is also an exile from progressive history, a feeling of being "out of joint" in time.[2]

In order to better understand the relation between the heterogeneity of Marti's discourse and the new, uncertain era it helps define, the present work begins with Ramos's sense of modernity as exile from progressive history, and then follows lines that have been set out by Jaime Rodríguez Matos, who considers the problem of time in his book *Writing the Formless: José Lezama Lima and the End of Time* (2017). My sense is that a "clash between the rhetoric of the Eternal Return and that of the *tabula rasa* of the New" is not only "a central matrix from which to make sense of the cultural politics of the Revolution," as Rodríguez Matos argues, but also the tension that defines Martí's diagnosis of his era (Rodríguez Matos, 31). The problematic of time and history as tension between eternal return and the radical break that is proclaimed by the New is intimately bound up with a feeling of exile from the city that brings him to refer to himself as "nature's son" (Ramos, xxxviii). Martí's work helps clarify how the problem of history in modernity is part and parcel with the ascendency of a concept of nature introduced by the romanticism of the late eighteenth century.

The question of history and its relation to nature becomes visible in the prologue to "Poema del Niágara" if one takes a step back to pay closer attention to the remarkable genealogy of Bonalde's poem, which has been largely ignored by scholars (including Martí, who only alludes to it indirectly in his prologue). "Poema del Niágara," first published in 1880, is actually the third in a series of poems about Niagara Falls written by Caribbean authors. In 1832, during his exile in the United States, José Maria Heredia wrote the poem "Niágara," describing the famous waterfall as an expression of America's natural prowess, revolutionary potential, and as the fount of its political independence. Then, in 1864, the Cuban poet Gertrudis Gómez de Avellaneda wrote "A vista de Niágara," responding to Heredia's poem by describing not only the Falls, but also a newly constructed bridge nearby—celebrating not only nature but also "industrial progress," and archiving a shift in value attending the epochal passage from romanticism to positivism. The poem by the Venezuelan writer strikes a strange relation to the two poems that precede it, repeating Avellaneda's difference with Heredia, but mentioning only the latter, more foundational writer. Investigating the "natural history" of the prologue—the complex relationship between the works that act as its condition of possibility and the understanding of nature that each expresses—qualifies Martí's reading of Bonalde's poem, and shows his position to be somewhat more troubling than Ramos's treatment does.

More than merely harkening to the romantic genre of the nature poem, Martí intricately expresses the nature ideology that it reinforces, and by which it was historically constituted. While stylistically one can see Martí's break with independence thinkers in the way Ramos describes, we also see in his work a recasting or reiteration of the vision of America as a state of nature set forth by the first wave of independence thinkers, which served as the main conceptual predicate of Latin American political and cultural autonomy.[3]

Martí's endorsement of Bonalde's poem mirrors the discursive and ideological function of nature insofar as it celebrates the Venezuelan author as someone who seeks simultaneously to fuse with the past and to destroy it. More than accurately portraying and introducing Bonalde's actual position, Martí's prologue must be read as an expression of his own paradoxical experience of being "out of joint" in time. He expresses this most clearly in an apparent contradiction between his act of calling for a renewal of the nature poem (which his endorsement performs) and his call for the destruction of old poetry in a bonfire toward the end of the prologue. It is precisely this kind of relation to history that the concept of nature reinforces, when it is taken as an imagination of a primordial space that stands outside the normal flow of time, and yet which is accessible within the present: a destruction of the past as a means of renewal (in the case of Latin America, its reinvention as a collection of nation-states). As such, the concept of nature holds the key to understanding the impossible tension between past, present, and future in Martí's work that Ramos illustrates. The prologue allows the reader to perceive the relation between an experience of being an exile from progressive history and the nature ideology that was developed during the late eighteenth and early nineteenth centuries.

Through the tremendous influence of his anti-imperial and prototypical decolonial thought, Martí ensured that a belief in the redemptive function of nature would remain an integral element of the Latin Americanism—or "nuestro americanismo"—he helped invent.[4] Consequently, he bears an oversized responsibility for the extent to which nature was mobilized as a conceptual tool for renewal and resistance in Latin America during the twentieth century and into the present day. His prologue to "Poema del Niágara" is a key document not only for understanding the nature thinking that informed much of his own work—"Nuestra América" and *Versos Sencillos* being the most obvious—but also the work of so many others who were influenced by him.

The beginning of Martí's prologue flatly denies any notion that Bonalde's decision to write another Latin American poem about Niagara Falls is unoriginal. Its opening line acknowledges this potential criticism to the reader who knows about the other Niagara Falls poems, but without fully illustrating or explaining it to a less knowledgeable one. Martí writes: "¡Éste que traigo de la mano no es zurcidor de rimas, ni repetidor de viejos maestros—que lo son porque nadie repitieron [. . .]: es Juan Antonio Pérez Bonalde, que ha escrito el 'Poema del Niágara'" ["The one I bring by the hand is no mender of old rhymes or repeater of old masters—who are masters because they never repeated anyone." No: "it is Juan Antonio Perez Bonalde, author of the 'Poema del Niagara'"] (21).

Though he does not mention him by name, the old master to which he refers here is Jose Maria Heredia, Cuban author of the first Niagara poem of 1832. A little further on he continues to consider Bonalde's relation to the unnamed master—whom he now refers to as a "giant"—and press the question of originality, writing:

> Y si me preguntas más de él, curioso pasajero, te diré que se midió con un gigante y no salió herido, sino con la lira bien puesta sobre el hombro. . . . Y no preguntes más, que ya es prueba sobrada de grandeza atreverse a medirse con gigantes; pues el mérito no está en el éxito del acometimiento, aunque éste volvió bien de la lid, sino en el valor de acometer. (21)
>
> [If you ask me more about him, curious passenger, I will tell you that he measured himself with a giant and came out not harmed, but rather, with his lyre firmly set upon his shoulder. . . . So don't ask me more: it is already exceeding sufficient proof of greatness to dare measure oneself against giants; and after all, the merit is not in the success of the attack—although this one returned safely from the battle—but rather the valor of the attacking.]

Whatever the true quality of Bonalde's poem may be, here Martí makes the claim that it is important to demonstrate bravery by challenging or attacking the heroes of the past, and then adds that the challenge itself is more important than it is to actually succeed in overcoming them. The first claim alone goes against a valuation of originality and newness that had characterized Latin American political romanticism up until this point, which, more than advocating measurement against the masters, often preferred to ignore them. The second claim radicalizes the first, and helps make it into an ethics.

In *The Latin American Mind* (1949) Leopoldo Zea elaborates the way in which this idea that the masters are great because they never "repeated" anyone—which Martí proclaims but then also seems to contradict in his advocacy of Bonalde—gained importance in early debates about how to define Latin American cultural autonomy. Regarding the newly independent Latin American culture, in 1842 José Victorino Lastárria writes "fuerza es que seamos originales" ("to be strong we must be original") echoing sentiments expressed by Esteban Echeverría a few years earlier when discussing the meter of *La cautiva* (1837): "Si el que imita a otro no es poeta, menos lo será el que, antes de darlo a luz, mutila su concepto para poderlo embutir en un patrón dado" ["If he who imitates another is not a poet, even less so will be one who, before bringing it to light, mutilates his concept to make it conform to a given pattern"] (119). Octavio Paz calls the development of this tendency in the twentieth century Latin America's "tradition of rupture" ("tradición de ruptura") (17).

Martí's approval of Bonalde's decision to write another poem about Niagara Falls is strange. For the contemporary reader who has probably only ever heard of Bonalde because of Martí's prologue, the claim that it is original seems to protest too much, and feels a little like an elaborate apology for the writing of another poem about the falls. From today's perspective, one can also sense how a proliferation of poems about the Falls might run parallel to their being made into a cliché, infinitely reproduced on postcards sold by the same tourism industry that built the city around it, which turned the Falls into anything but wild, a parody of what nature is "supposed" to be. Furthermore, Martí's celebration of the poem seems like contradiction of his claim that one must never repeat the past. Even if Bonalde's poem does in fact challenge Heredia (and I will argue that it does further on), after Martí proclaims its originality, his description of it makes it seem like mere repetition. He does not call attention to any difference between the poems, or to how exactly Bonalde attacks Heredia. He repeats the tropes one would expect—the exalted power of the falls, the lyricism they inspire—and even uses the adjective "Heredian" ["herediano"] to describe Bonalde's prose (in the only explicit reference to Cuban master), effectively negating his claim that the Venezuelan poet doesn't repeat (33).

Then, to conclude his promotion of Bonalde's poem, Martí insists on its taking part in a modern claim of rupture that calls for a radical break with the past.

> Pon de lado las huecas rimas de uso, ensartadas de perlas y matizadas con flores de artificio, que suelen ser más juego de la mano y divertimiento de ocioso ingenio que llamarada del alma y hazaña digna de los magnates de la mente. Junta en haz alto, y echa al fuego, pesares de contagio, tibiedades latinas, rimas reflejas, dudas ajenas, males de libros, fe prescrita, caliéntate a la llama saludable del frío de estos tiempos dolorosos. (39)

> [Put aside the hollow, used up rhymes, encrusted with pearls and colored with flowers of artifice, which tend to be more slight of hand and diversion of idle invention than the flaring of the soul, or achievement worthy of the magnates of the mind. Gather into a tall heap and put to flame contagious sorrows, lukewarm Latinities, reflected rhymes, foreign doubts, ills of books, prescribed

> faith—warm yourself on the healthy flame against the cold of these painful times.]

Against any repetition of the past, or recollection of the masters, Martí calls for their destruction in a bonfire.

In light of this call to burn the "used up rhymes" of yesteryear, what is one to make of his praise for Bonalde's poem, which clearly goes back to a poem that had been used at least twice already—once by Heredia and once by Avellaneda—if only to measure himself against it? How does one reconcile Martí's call to burn poetry past in a bonfire with his celebration of Bonalde's Heredian prose? We are faced with the confusion Ramos describes, a tension between a harkening to the past and a call to break with it.

One interpretation would maintain that the work of Heredia simply does not fall into the group of things Martí would see burned in a bonfire. While latinities, used up rhymes, and the ills of books must be discarded, Heredia is a revolutionary poet who should be remembered and emulated.

But this explanation does not address the extent to which the issue of imitation and originality was just as concerning for Martí as it was for his predecessors. Other works by the Cuban thinker lead one to believe that even though he admired Heredia, he would never want another poet to copy him. The motif regarding originality and imitation—visible in an opposition between the imported book and nature in "Nuestra America"—is characterized by Rodríguez Matos as the opposition between the "copista," who can only imitate, and the poet, who creates spontaneously. The *copista* is "a cultural functionary who operates via *imitation*, reproducing cultural models that already exist and have a generally accepted value ascribed to them. Against this kind of copyist, he proposes another: 'When ideas are ripe for expression, they come of their own accord . . . when he who would be their vehicle does not expect it'" (Rodríguez Matos, 57). This "other," the poet, is a conduit of nature, whose work arises spontaneously, as the fruit of a tree ripens, without artifice, and without resorting to imitation. It is clear that Martí heavily favors the latter figure. After all, it is precisely because he does not imitate that the nature poet will free America from its dependency on European culture, and allow it to be culturally and politically autonomous. In light of this motif, Martí's celebration of Bonalde's reinscription of the Niagara Falls poem cannot simply be explained by his respect for Heredia's greatness.

Jorge Luis Borges's thinking about imitation and originality can shed some light on the paradox of Martí's celebration of "Poema de Niagara," and his sense that it is not unoriginal. In a certain way, Martí's resembles the fictional narrator of "Pierre Menard, autor del Quijote" (1939), who celebrates the eponymous intellectual's claim of having written several sections of *Don Quijote* again.[5] Just as Menard's *Quixote* is not less original than

Cervantes's and is in fact superior—"el texto de Cervantes y el de Menard son verbalmente idénticos, pero el segundo es casi infinitamente más rico" ["Cervantes's text and Menard's are verbally identical, but the second is almost infinitely richer"]—according to the narrator, Bonalde does not repeat per se ("ni repetidor de viejos maestros") by writing another Latin American exile poem about Niagara Falls (*Ficciones*, 45; *Labyrinths*, 42). Understanding what Menard hopes to accomplish by writing the *Quixote* again can provide an answer to why Martí celebrates Bonalde's "repetition" of poems by Heredia and Avellaneda as something other than repetition.

The narrator explains that Menard chooses to write Cervantes's *magnum opus* because "El *Quijote* es un libro contingente, el *Quijote* es innecesario" ["The *Quixote* is a contingent book; the *Quixote* is unnecessary"] (*Ficciones*, 43; *Labyrinths*, 41). The importance of its contingency is illuminated toward the end of the fiction, when Menard is quoted as saying: "Todo hombre debe ser capaz de todas las ideas y entiendo que en el porvenir lo será" ["Every man should be capable of all ideas and I understand that in the future this will be the case"] (*Ficciones*, 48; *Labyrinths*, 44). These two statements lead the reader to assume that Menard ascribes to the positivist belief in the possibility of developing a hard social science of history (or in this case, story) that would allow for a precise prediction of future events, and which will ultimately result in the equality of all men. He is a caricature of the utopian positivist (and perhaps more specifically a Marxist Hegelian), taking his belief in the power of science to the logical extreme. By replicating the creation of the most contingent book, Menard would prove that even the most aleatory event can be reduced to a kind of scientific determinism. The repetition of the novel can be read as being akin to the repetition of an experiment in a lab, one that would make literature—and by extension human history—no longer a subject of contingency. Thus, Menard is a kind of scientific prophet, who seeks to prove the imminence of (and to help bring about) the end of history.

By spontaneously reproducing Cervantes's most important work, Menard will displace and supersede the mythical Spanish writer, rendering his genius obsolete by demonstrating in the most radical way possible that all men are capable of all ideas. He rewrites the *Quixote* in order to prove that it is no longer necessary. He repeats the history in order to do away with it.

Through "Pierre Menard" we can understand Martí's celebration of "Poema del Niágara" not as a repetition that remembers Heredia, but rather as an "original repetition" that forgets him: a repetition that supersedes the original. I sense that Martí wishes to imagine Bonalde as a new Heredia in the present, taking his place and rendering him obsolete and dispensable. "Poema del Niágara" would take the place previously held by "Niágara," as the rebirth or renewal of the older poem for the next generation under the guise of spontaneous originality. As with Menard, Bonalde's rewriting would challenge and displace the past by reconstituting it.

In this Menardian reading, it is crucial that Bonalde evokes Heredia in particular. Heredia is a founding father of independent national Latin American literary expression, and his importance in Cuba is not unlike that of Cervantes in Spain. This not only lends credence to a reading of Bonalde as a living Menard, but calls attention to the Oedipal overtones of the displacement he ostensibly performs. His secret motivation is to take the place of the father—in this case, the father of independent Latin American culture.

With this realization one begins to suspect that Bonalde is really a stand-in for Martí—an expression of the Cuban's Oedipal desire—and that the displacement he ascribes to Bonalde is really the one he wishes to perform himself. It is not hard to see the personal and intellectual affinities between Martí and Heredia: how the former took up the cause of the latter, brought it to fruition, and became the new nature poet of Cuban independence.[6] If anyone repeats and displaces Heredia, it is Martí.

Years before, Heredia expressed his political aspirations for Cuban independence from Spain as being bound up with a view of America as a site of a nature, which he represented repeatedly as a place standing outside and against history. In an early poem "En el teocalli de Cholula" (1820), Heredia stands on a ruined pyramid in Mexico, a relic of an older indigenous empire, and thinks about those other indigenous civilizations whose presence on the land have been erased completely by the destructive forces of nature. He imagines the Spanish empire one day becoming like these lost civilizations, vanishing and making way for a new order, which is none other than the autonomous national republic for which he was fighting. "Niagara" maintains a similar view of nature as a space of timelessness that might be mobilized as a means of political renewal. The Falls represent the hope that man might begin anew and forget his past. The particularity of its manifestation of nature seems to help inspire the greatness of the North American people, who had already ceased to be a colony and attained independence. Heredia contrasts its cold, bracing force to the lazy palm trees of the Caribbean, ascribing a kind of geographical determinism to U.S. independence.

Just as it is significant that the book that Menard writes is the *Quixote* insofar as he comes to resemble its crazed protagonist, it is significant that the poem that Bonalde renews is, as Martí writes, the "extraordinary and resplendent song of the inexhaustible poem of nature" insofar as the function of the modern concept of nature is to erase history (31). If Martí is really suggesting that Bonalde could displace Heredia, the philosophy of destructive renewal he expresses would have to be understood as a development of the same romantic nature ideology that Heredia himself developed and promoted. For Martí, Bonalde's rewriting of Heredia's poem is not just a return to Niagara Falls, but also a return to the romantic nature of Latin American independence: a return to the return to nature. Like Heredia did before him, Martí casts this return to nature precisely as an escape from history, an alternative to past, present, and future. In the prologue he writes:

> lo pasado, ¡todo es castillo solitario y armadura vacía; lo presente, ¡todo es pregunta, negación, cólera, blasfemia de derrota, alarido de triunfo!, lo venidero, ¡todo está oscurecido en el polvo y vapor de la batalla! Y fatigado de buscar en vano hazañas en los hombres, fue el poeta a saludar la hazaña de la naturaleza. (32)
>
> [[t]he past, with lonely castles and empty armor!; the present, with questions, negations, anger, blasphemy of defeat, cries of victory!; the future, obscured in the dust and fog of battle! Tired of vain searching amid the triumphs of men, the poet [i.e., Bonalde] went to greet the triumph of nature.]

It is with this return to a nature previously mobilized as an alternative to history—a return to the *same* nature, that is, Niagara Falls, by the same means, the nature poem—that Bonalde would ostensibly escape the law of Latin American cultural history as Heredia defined it, while at the same time being ironically bound to it in repetition.

Few critics who write about Martí's prologue fail to mention that Bonalde's posterity does not live up to the praise he receives. Yet, it is not readily recognized that Marti's reading overpowers the young writer's poem, and that perhaps his effusive praise is not carried out in good faith. Far from seeking to erase history or burn the past in a bonfire, Bonalde frames "Poema del Niágara" as a pilgrimage to Heredia's Niagara. Against Martí's claim that Bonalde does not repeat old masters, the poem is explicitly concerned with the repetition that occurs when the poet goes to pay homage to the Cuban master, whom he names in the first stanza.[7]

If any master gets "Menarded" by Bonalde's poem—and Martí's reading of it—it is Avellaneda, and her "A vista de Niágara." Without ever mentioning her, Bonalde's Niagara Falls poem repeats the sentiment expressed by her earlier poem: both its performance of pilgrimage and its qualification of Heredia's romantic understanding of nature.

Avellaneda conspicuously differs with Heredia's superlative treatment of the Falls as a god. Heredia, on the one hand, persistently suggests the divinity of the Falls in the romantic fashion, shouting "omnipotente Dios" ("omnipotent God") in his address, and closes by comparing his own frailty and mortality to its power and everlastingness (Heredia, 142).[8] Avellaneda, on the other hand turns to a recently constructed bridge at the end of her poem and cries: "¡Salve, o aéreo, indescribible puente,/Obra del hombre, que emular procuras/La obra de Dios, junto á la cuál te ostentas!/¡Salve, signo valiente/Del progreso industrial" ["Hail, oh aerial and indescribable bridge, work of man that succeeds in emulating the work of God, alongside which you exhibit yourself. Hail, brave sign of industrial progress!"] (374). Here it is not the Falls that is like a god, but rather man, whose dominion over nature, facilitated by the union of science and technology, was growing dramatically during this period of the nineteenth century.

Although Bonalde makes no mention of Avellaneda, he also searches for Heredia's God in the Falls ("do te ocultas deidad tronadora" ["where are you hiding, thundering diety"]), shouting to it as Heredia did, but receives no response beside the echo of his own voice (161). Here, like Avellaneda, Bonalde invokes the disenchantment of the modern world, if not proclaiming man's supremacy over the god nature as Avellaneda seems to do, at least observing that he has been left to fend for himself, that his own voice is the only one available for providing answers to his spiritual torment. He reflects: "tu no eres más que yo, ni más que el hombre! / Tú eres la imagen viva / De la proscrita humanidad altiva; / Tú eres el hombre mismo. . . . Nada supiste responderme, nada; / Que lo que el hombre ignora / Lo ingoras tú también" ["You are not greater than me, nor than man; / you are the living image / of haughty, banished humanity; / you are man himself . . . / you knew nothing to answer me; /what man knows not /you know not as well"] (177–78). The Falls echo the poet and are "proscribed" like a man in political exile: their outward appearance of confidence and power conceal hidden hollows of doubt and ignorance. If they are a god, they are a powerless one.

Martí's prologue does not acknowledge that the doubt racking Bonalde's poem is in fact a doubt about nature itself: doubt about the divinity of the Falls and their ability to provide the kind of solution to the political imperatives of the day that Heredia had hoped they would. To question the divinity of the falls is to question the divinity of the nature they stand for and the function it was supposed to serve in postenlightenment thought. Even as Bonalde attempts to move beyond a romantic understanding of nature, Marti's prologue "corrects" his poem, restoring the older, Heredian meaning of the Falls. He prefers to see the young poet's return to Niagara as a return to purity, truth, and spirituality—nature as "the only legitimate theme of modern poetry," as a modern god (Martí, 29). Martí canonizes an inverted interpretation of the poem, adulterating Bonalde's memory within Latin American letters, perhaps irrevocably.

Although he will mainly be remembered as the forgotten poet of Marti's prologue, Bonalde achieves something significant in challenging the ideology of nature that the Falls represent. Yet, he nevertheless reinscribes that same ideology which he attempts to critique, failing to acknowledge the literary history subsequent to the Heredian origin of independent Latin American literature, and ignoring his repetition of Avellaneda's return. His desire for the origin still causes him to repeat history, though not the one he thinks he does.

This kind of ongoing amnesiac repetition and misreading that seeks to simultaneously restore an original truth and obliterate it is deeply symptomatic of the system of belief that the idea of nature itself reinforces. The echoing relation between Heredia, Avellaneda, Bonalde, and Martí shows the history of Latin American literature becoming the history of a repetition of the same return to nature: the search for a break with tradition that merely affirms that tradition with greater force every time it is carried out.

There can be little question that a fantasy of nature—of a place that stands outside the flow of history, but which reinforces its repetition through the erasure of history—is ideology as Foucault understood it: the belief that conditions thought without making its presence known, and which causes the thinker to betray his own intentions. This sense of ideology as blindness—a "pattern of self-mystification that accompanies the experience of crisis"—is what is at stake when, in reference to the Cuban revolutionary impulse, Rodríguez Matos describes his desire to comprehend the "underlying structure that sends us in an endless circle, in which the solution reproduces the problems it was supposed to correct" (De Man, 16; Rodríguez Matos, 59). It is the structure that Borges describes in "Pierre Menard." Beyond the patent impossibility of Menard's project, and the fact that its realization could never be proved, with his attempt to write the *Quixote*, he comes to resemble its crazed protagonist. He repeats the *Quixote* insofar as he acts out its story, which recounts the adventures of a madman who tries to remake a fantastical past within the present. Menard is doubly foolish, not only trying to carry out an impossible task, but also failing to appreciate a basic lesson of the book he wants to overcome.

But Martí's prologue shows something more than the blindness and unwitting error that the ideology of nature reinforces. While Martí misreads Bonalde's poem, it is hard to believe that this misreading is entirely unintentional. The misreading does not undermine Martí's cause but rather furthers it, helping to create a space for him within the intellectual patriarchy of Latin America. He demonstrates a surprisingly accurate and frank understanding of nature as a concept whose function is to erase the past, and he embraces it for precisely this reason. Martí's nature is the destruction of the archive, the bonfire in which the law is burned, and as such a means for effectuating a displacing, supersessionary maneuver for the realization of his will to power. The prologue expresses a fantasy of being the new Heredia and helps make it into a reality. It is impossible to know the extent of Martí's *agency* in this expression of an Oedipal desire to displace Heredia, and his use of nature to assist in this operation—whether he fully grasps what he is doing—but its precision cannot be denied. Martí's is a moment in which a Foucaultian understanding of the decentralized and agentless operation of ideology/power meets the centralized, personal will to power.

NOTES

1. It is a tradition in Martí criticism to try to pinpoint the way in which he was a prophet of modernity. In "Una aproximación existencial al << Prólogo al *Poema del Niágara*>> de Jose Martí" (1973), Jose Olivio Jimenez describes how the romanticism within Martí's thinking "impulsa a la moderna conciencia existencial" ["drives the modern existential consciousness"] (410). José Miguel Oviedo in *Breve historia del ensayo hispanoamericano* (1990) states that the prologue "constituye la primera definición del espíritu modernista en América" ["constitutes the primary definition of the modernist spirit in America"] (38). Miguel Gomes cites this essay in "La nostalgia modernista del centro: dos Prologos," and expands on the connections between Martí, Darío, and Nietzsche. See also "El Prólogo al *Poema del Niágara* de José Martí y la revolución modernista" (1995) by Ángel Esteban and "El poeta y el cronista modernista en el Prólogo al Poema del Niágara" (2016) by Jaime Galgani Muñoz.

2. The phrase "time is out of joint" is taken from Shakespeare's *Hamlet* as used by Jacques Derrida in *Specters of Marx* (1994) to think about the uneasy relationship between the intellectual and those who preceded him—on the one hand Derrida and Marx, but then also Marx and Hegel. It is precisely Hamlet's uneasy relationship with his father's ghost that defines his feeling that time is out of joint.

3. While various independence thinkers maintained qualitatively different understandings of nature, they tended to agree that it was a space of historical oblivion. Andrés Bello and Domingo Faustino Sarmiento, for example, maintained antithetical views of nature, the former seeing it as a paradisaical space and the latter understanding it as a nightmarish, barbaric desert. Nevertheless, both maintained it as the *tabula rasa* that would serve as a vital resource for transitioning out of the Spanish Empire, allowing for the creation of a new, independent nation-state completely free from the colonial past.

4. Describing Martí as the "spiritual father of the revolution," Jaime Rodríguez Matos traces his legacy within the *foquismo* of the Cuban revolutionary tradition through Vitier and Guevara in his book *Writing of the Formless* (56). He develops an understanding of the influence of his romantic belief in nature, observing the way in which for both Martí and Guevara "the idealism of the Revolution has to become a force of nature, sprouting wild, without being cultivated" (60). In *The Limits of Identity: Politics and Poetics in Latin America* (2015) Charles Hatfield describes the legacy of Martí's "nuestra americanismo" within the larger phenomenon of a Latin Americanism defined by the claim of difference. "'Nuestra América' has been mobilized both as the forerunner of South Asian postcolonial theory and an organic Latin American theoretical alternative to it, and it has served as a model for what José David Saldívar calls 'comparative cultural studies.' Indeed, 'Nuestra América' is repeatedly held up as a fresh, new roadmap for the Latin American future or as an unfinished project whose state of unfinishedness defines the present tasks of Latin Americanism" (Hatfield, 12). The "decolonial" movement led by Walter Mignolo is the latest of these projects that seek to fulfill this incomplete decolonization of Latin American thought.

5. "No quería componer otro Quijote—lo cual es fácil—sino *el Quijote*. Inútil agregar que no encaró nunca una transcripción mecánica del original; no se proponía copiarlo. Su admirable ambición era producir unas páginas que coincidieran—palabra por palabra y línea por línea—con las de Miguel de Cervantes" (*Ficciones*, 41).

"He did not want to compose another *Quixote*—which is easy—but *the Quixote itself.* Needless to say, he never contemplated a mechanical transcription of the original; he did not propose to copy it. His admirable intention was to produce a few pages which would coincide—word for word and line for line—with those of Miguel de Cervantes" (*Labyrinths* 39).

6. Martí sings his praises in the essay "Heredia" (1889).

7. A few years after Martí writes his prologue, Nietzsche shows it is better not to name the master you wish to supersede. In *Twilight of the Idols* (1888) Nietzsche describes himself as a destroyer of the idols that uphold the "slave morality" of Judaism and Christianity—that is, as one who will philosophize with a hammer. Without naming him, he casts himself as Abraham (the patriarch of the morality he claims to destroy), who smashed the clay figures his father made and sold. Despite the irony of this act of casting himself after the Jewish patriarch he claims to overturn, we must believe that Nietzsche understands what he is doing, because he

explores an almost identical supersessionary gesture—how Paul invents the Christian religion as supersession of Judaism, as its fulfillment and displacement—in *The Anti-Christ* (1895).

8. In *Natural Supernaturalism* (1971) M. H. Abrams considers the discursive event in which the romantic concept of nature takes on the qualities previously ascribed to God, reflecting a "secularization of inherited theological ideas and ways of thinking" that Theodor Adorno and Max Horkheimer describe in *Dialectic of Enlightenment* (12).

WORKS CITED

Abrams, M. H. *Natural Supernaturalism: Tradition and Revolution in Romantic Literature*. Norton, 1971.

Avellaneda, Gertrudis Gómez de. "A vista de Niágara." *Poes ías líricas*. L. Lopez, 1877.

Borges, Jorge Luis. "Pierre Menard, autor del Quijote." *Ficciones*. Planeta DeAgostini, 2000.

———. "Pierre Menard, Author of the Quixote." *Labyrinths*. Translated by James E. Irby. New Directions, 1962.

De Man, Paul. *Blindness and Insight*. Methuen, 1983.

Derrida, Jacques. *Specters of Marx*. Routledge, 1994.

Echeverría, Esteban. *El matadero-La cautiva*. Catedra, 2003.

Gomes, Miguel. "La nostalgia modernista del centro: dos Prologos." *Ciberletras* 4 (2001).

Hatfield, Charles. *The Limits of Identity: Politics and Poetics in Latin America*. University of Texas Press, 2015.

Heredia, José María. "Niágara." *Niágara y otros textos*, edited by Ángel Augier. Biblioteca Ayacucho, 1990.

Horkheimer, Max, and Theodor W. Adorno. *Dialectic of Enlightenment: Philosophical Fragments*. 1947. Stanford University Press, 2007.

Jimenez, Jose Olivio. "Una aproximación existencial al <<Prólogo al *Poema del Niágara*>> de José Martí." *Anales de la literatura hispanoamericana*. 16 (1973–74): 407–42.

Lastárria, José Victorino. *Discursos académicos de J.V. Lastarria*. Impr. del Siglo, 1844.

Martí, José. "Prólogo al 'Poema del Niágara' de Juan A. Pérez Bonalde." *Ensayos y crónicas*, edited by José Olivio Jiménez. Anaya & Mario Muchnik, 1995.

Nietzsche, Friedrich. *Twilight of the Idols and the Anti-Christ*. Penguin, 2003.

Oviedo, José Miguel. *Breve historia del ensayo hispanoamericano*. Alianza, 1990.

Paz, Octavio. *Hijos del limo*. Seix Barral, 1981.

Pérez Bonalde, Juan A. *Ritmos*. "Poema del Niágara." New York, 1880.

Ramos, Julio. *Divergent Modernities*. Translated by John D. Blanco. Duke University Press, 2001.

Rodríguez Matos, Jaime. *Writing of the Formless: José Lezama Lima and the End of Time*. Fordham University Press, 2017.

Chapter Three

Men and Women of the Earth in the Texts of Martí's Travels

Mayra Beatriz Martínez,
Translated by Stephanie Thom

I talk to you of what I have always spoken to you about: of this unknown giant, of these babbling lands, of our fabulous America.

—*José Martí*

Letter de Valero Pujol, 27 November 1877

Throughout[1] his haphazard life, and especially during his travels through America, José Martí wrote various kinds of texts. The record of his travel experiences is found primarily in the newspapers for which he wrote. In their monumental chronicles, these travel writings were able to carry the elements in Martí's advanced political project and contributed to the revolution of an American mode of writing. However, unfairly silenced by the overwhelming preeminence of his travel writings—widely known, even in his time—is a prose medium of notable transcendence, writings of an even more personal character in which can be found the most immediate and spontaneous fruits of his *American Journeys*: diaries, notepads, and memoirs. In these testimonies of his travels are topics hardly explored even by the most ardent critic, which, nevertheless, could result in understanding how Martí the man came to the genesis—imperfect, doubtful, contradictory on occasion—of his mature ideas. These texts offer distinctive messages outside of the official culture largely from communities far from the city centers. Martí's record—a reconstruction of a collective experience produced in the vicinity of those marginalized contexts of power, either by reason of class, race, or gender—is essentially marked by the call for justice and the visceral commitment to establishing social equality. The texts compose a literary corpus that openly reflects the process of Martí's thinking, encompassing and analyzing data, giving priority to conforming factors of American society found from social practice; I will discuss the basis of Martí's accumulated observations and try to suggest how the author carried forward his sociocultural project. This chapter will focus on "Mother America" (1889), the essay "Our America" (1891), and the *Manifesto of Montecristi* (1895); the significance of these works is found in the moments which are anchored thematically in the most authentic reality of "the romantic nations of the continent" and "the painful islands of the sea" (Martí, 23), including Cuba.

Martí could not avoid a doctrinal mindset in his travel journals: practically none of us are free of acute digressions, which depart from daily observations and conceptualize and fix prescriptions around the most dissimilar aspects of life. It wasn't for leisure that Martí asserted, during an interview for *Revista Universal* in 1875, that "experience is the strongest base of knowledge. . . . The good reason . . . analyzes everything you feel: study everything you see" (Martí, 333–34).

In examining the phenomena that he is finding and in his coexistence with the groups he has just encountered, the author-witness annotates and describes dialectically, that is to say in pursuit of generalizations: eventually—now that enough time has elapsed—we can recognize, in those elements, specific cultural factors of the places he visited. Before, we could speculate that Martí had a profound perception in regard to the selection of members of the community and their general traits and representations that identified them. Because these traits were important, they were expressed more visibly by people in each community and were, in the end, the traits transmitted from generation to generation. To a large extent, these attributes determined the peculiarities of the group: turns of speech, diet, and objects representative of their material culture—housing construction, instruments, dresses, ornaments—as well as elements inherent in their subjectivity: their arts, their cosmologies, and the ethical values that govern their lives or the reasons for their more ancestral customs—that is, their spirituality. The witness-Martí will reflect on these attributes by putting them properly in relation to various economies. Thus, he will interpret them as cultural responses of adaptation to the environment and not simply as typical features orchestrated to form a customary stamp.

We must recognize, however, that regionalist stereotyping—implicit in the literary nationalism of the Spanish colonies' independence processes—is part of his travel notes, published in the *Revista Universal* in December 1876.[2] This corresponds to the beginning of his Mexican period, when he was ecstatic that America revealed the "art of centuries, of ages" and in which the picturesque "Indian, of blue shawl, offers a basket of pomegranates through the window."[3] But then he wonders still, unable to answer questions about land ownership and the distance between native peoples and the legacy of colonialism. Months later, we see him still clinging to a lavish but nonetheless superficial view of those people, which fails to explain them. In the notes made during his transit from Havana in March 1877, heading to Guatemala, he describes the following:

> Here on this vast sand, of torment to the feet and white death of the waves, furnished in broken shells, sprinkled with huts of nice roofs of braided leaves, glossed with sturdy natives, here among these careless men, between these streets, on this grateful sand that does not stifle the foreigner who steps on it, here rests my soul, mistress of fatigue, content with the serenity of this greatness, populated and comforted in the midst of this lonely pier. (Martí, C.E., 15)

In a letter to Manuel Mercado, from *Progreso* and dated February 28, 1877, related to a projected book that could be the one to which these quotes correspond (Martí, C.E., 34), Martí makes a statement illustrating his writing process: "I write on the run of the pen, a book of thought and narration. *More than what I see, I tell what I think*" (Martí, C.E., 29), which denounces, to some extent, a biased reflection capable of weighing down his apprehension of the human and natural landscapes with which he stumbles for the first time. At the same time—and independently—he speaks of how "the soul grows in grandeur in the contemplation of the natures greatness" (Martí, C.E., 29). He not only speaks separately of his appreciation of man and nature that surrounds him, but even, at times, he opposes them: "This is land sown with thistles, but enameled with good hearts" (Martí, C.E., 29).

This critical awareness in his message, it seems, quickly put him at the door of less a priori thinking, and asks him to gain a more objective knowledge from experience as "the firmest base of knowledge," resulting from the study of "everything he sees" (Martí, 333–34), as he had warned since 1875. Only a month later, he expresses a nascent desire to explain precise details of what he observed, composing a sociopsychological space of belonging that could reinforce the concerns of those towns.[4] In March 1877, as Martí passes through Holbox, he considers for the first time an idea that will be indispensable to his understanding. From the beginning we can see a significant focus on human activity as an expression of the possibilities that its environment offers. The correspondence between man and the natural environment in which he is born and lives—and with which it necessarily establishes a link limited by the satisfaction of vital necessities of life—will justly and inevitably become a distinctive cultural stamp: man responds materially and spiritually to that nature:

> Coming from Progreso to the Island of Women, one passes very close to Contoy. Jolbós is a small village of fishermen, much less important than the island, frequented only by *coyucos* or small canoes, where they trade turtles and dogfish. There is not only the fishing village, there are also cornfields,

> poor haciendas, and these fruits and fish are sold by the inhabitants in the towns of the coast, and mainly in Progreso to Mérida. The greatest wealth in Jolbós, consists of a cornfield, a house with a little gate, and one or two canoes. This brings together the producer, the consignee and the trader in the same hand. (Martí, 25)

Martí's "The Diary of Izabal to Zacapa" of 1877 declares similar concerns: he does not conceal his interest in consigning the particular way of life of the human groups, mainly concentrating on the relation between the economic and the cultural. In this way, very eloquently, he starts the text addressed to his close friends, the Valdés Domínguez brothers:

> In Zacapa they live mainly on tobacco and hats (*de los sombreros de petate*): this is the *patrimony*, as the people of the people would say. Trade, almost nonexistent abroad; by its scarce outward forms, however at the same time, active. Here they come from all the nearby valleys, to be filled with all kinds of necessities.—In the form that almost all the houses of the people are deposits for sugar, liquor, fabrics, iron, ceramics, primitive articles crucial for the poor life of the fields. (Martí, C. E., 51)

Later his texts move beyond the simple chain of fortuitous facts and experiences and become endorsers of processes that decided, to a great extent, the Latin American destinies of today. To this end, they would be fed the most diverse angles of a modern reality, which became increasingly chaotic and fragmentary, although they would always pay for that peculiar reception of the man-nature bond which he already glimpsed and which he would clearly allude to in his "Prologue to the Poem of Niagara" by Pérez Bonalde, when he referred to "the prophetic and very soft insight of the rebellious and ignorant man and the fatal and revelatory nature" (Martí, 223). The traveler Martí, in the records of his pilgrimages through American lands and in directing his interest gradually toward the cultural result of this relationship, will go in pursuit of defining a discourse of cultural identity, perhaps not yet fully sensitive to its communities of origin—particularly Indians, blacks, and mestizos—where the "natural man" lived in circumstances where certain Latin American people were still in quest of emancipation.[5] In this way, at the same time, the Brazilian Milton Santos wrote: "Culture is the form of communication of the individual and of the social group with the universe, seeing it as an inheritance and as a relearning of the deep relations between man and his environment" (Mateo, 10).

It must be said, then, that Martí demonstrates an advanced approach to the subject. He offers a considerable contribution in the nineteenth century to the conclusion that "the whole story is only the narration of the work of adjustment, and the combats, between extra-human Nature and human Nature," according to the document of unknown dates (Martí, 44). That is not how it was usually understood then. Until Romanticism, at least in literature, the individual is a passive being confronting fatal nature that had touched him at birth. However, even for the romantic Martí, we see in the early notes of his travel journal *La Havana a Progreso* that man establishes a dialogue of equals with nature:

> I measure my greatness by the irritated oceans: when I traveled in the powerful Celtic, vessel of immigrants and Princes, I saw—and not in the Princes—more respectable heroes, the Black Atlantic gathered all the forces of his bosom, his dilated body could not fit in the relentless shore of their seas, and writhed with mountains-shaking, asking for strength to heaven, black too and dark, as the forehead of a sad father, who wants to stop with his wrath the impatience of a revolted son. Sea looks to the sky, there in the vastness of the horizon. I never felt terror before such great struggles; before, in the maw, firmly in the orbits my eyes, king among such majesty, my back felt Herculean. A religious spirit transported me; I wanted to battle, my home, I believed was that black space and deep ship, and rejoiced as a child, I adored that danger, that at last, I knew and looked at the sky high, which is my way of painting on my knees. (Martí, 16)

It will not be long before Martí begins, likewise, to appreciate humanity as a transformer: able to receive nature but also to contribute to its beneficial or detrimental action. Referring to the virgin islet of Conty, he notes the predatory actions of occasional visitors: "At times, sailors come down to the coast, wield a stick, and such is the abundance of the compact masses of birds, which in blows kill and injure hundreds of them" (Martí, 25). Days later, in the text "Island of Women," Martí establishes the need for harmony between civilization and nature as a topic: "Alas! Unhappy is the old who has not fulfilled the precept of the Arab: this man has not made a book, he has not planted a tree, he has not cured a son."[6]

The singular way in which Martí deals with the man-nature relationship becomes even more important in the subsequent narration of his first trip to Guatemala and in his reflections after a stay of a little more than a year. In the successive notes collected under the titles "Livingston" and "The Diary of Izabal to Zacapa" (both from March 1877), his reflections on what has happened extend to certain moments of his impressions of America ("Impressions of America")—published in English, in 1880—and to his memoirs "The Central America" ("L'Amerique centrale") and "The Disorders of the Republics of Central America" ("Les troubles des républiques de Amérique Centrale")—originally written in French and appearing to date back to 1882. They are illustrative of a well-defined stage for the life and work of the writer where Martí manages to fully recognize how the subsistence of man, linked to a context with specific conditions, obliges him to use natural resources in a certain way, which determines the peculiar economy of each group and is reflected in their conduct and their traditional knowledge. In the records from his visit to Livingston, this different point of view is already announced:

> The house is poor, but clean: the hammocks are of white canvas; spotless containers for water; new and well braided basket, walls covered with yellow pastry, and huddled with beautiful coconuts in the corner. From that they lived; coconut, cassava, banana. . . . These Caribs of ample heart are the cultivators of the fields; men fish and trade; women sow and make their trade of mothers and wives. The same hands that introduce to the earth the stem, then pluck its juicy root, and give it to the traveler in broad cake. (Martí, C.E., 49)

Obviously, the traveler-Martí then surpasses his initial ethical-aesthetic perspective, which only allowed him to reach an emotional approach, to stop in the objective-essential bonds that unite man with his environment. Interestingly, Martí's text is marked by the healing of that human relationship with the environment—not already with nature as an idyllic scenario—and, from that level of higher understanding, it underscores the need for that link to be "natural" (i.e., authentic and legitimate, not artificial and imposed). Thus, it begins to recognize the transformative role of the individual: a human-nature interactivity, which generates every particular culture.

It is imperative that we offer a side note here to clarify what we can understand as a "natural" man or woman, a concept that we mentioned earlier linked to Martí's definition of the identity discourse of different marginalized communities that he knows—Indians, blacks, and mestizos—and that it is indispensable to understand the reason for Martí's concern for achieving a proper authenticity of the man-nature relationship. Martí uses those terms explicitly in his master essay "Our America" of 1891, when he states:

> That's why the imported book has been defeated in America by the natural man. Natural men have defeated the artificial lawyers. The native mestizo has defeated the exotic Creole. There is no battle between civilization and barbarism, but between false erudition and nature. (Martí, 17)

Apart from this reflection, more than once he wanted to identify the "natural man," directly and exclusively, with "indigenous mestizo" (Martí, 17). This thought may well be broader if we realize that "nature" is the one that governs the "indigenous mestizo" while the "false erudition" is attributed, therefore, to "exotic Creole," to the "artificial lawyer" of the city (Martí, 17). But can nature determine only the "indigenous half-breed"? (Martí, 17). In fact, at other times, Martí has extended the condition of "natural" to what has the condition of "legitimate"—"How is it *natural religion* that rebels against nature?" What is the *legitimate religion* that stands against the law? How is it natural, how is it "lawful that religion commands the man to rebel against the precept of his God?" (Martí, 17). In 1894, in his book of notes, number 18, Martí came to categorically assert: "Natural thing to be Indian" (Martí, 384). But, moreover, in reading "Our America" with some detail, we can infer that, according to Martí, "natural statesmen" should thaw "natural blood," studying "nature," learning "Indian," with "nature" and "Indian" as synonymous (Martí, 21). Let us remember: "With the fire of the heart, thaw the coagulated America! To cast, to bull and to bounce, through the veins, the *natural blood* of the country. . . . *Natural statesmen* of the direct study of *nature* arise [and ends the paragraph]. The governors, *in the republics of Indians, learn Indian nature*" (Martí, 21). In his memoirs of the "Voyage of Izabal to Zacapa," he reaffirms the Indian to the category of "natural." He writes: "The Totopoxte, a symbol of strength, has gone to seek a *natural job*:—Lola!" She looks like a *corn-woman* (Martí, C.E., 77). Years later, in "A Trip to Venezuela," Martí reiterates his fascination related to the survival of the indigenous universe:

> Socialist Solutions, born of the European ills, have nothing to cure in the Amazon jungle, where the wild divinities are still worshipped. It is there that we must study, *in the book of nature, together in those miserable huts*. An agricultural country needs an agricultural education. (Martí, 160)

Again, on April 8, 1895, from Haiti, Martí reflects: "By the power of resistance of the *Indian* it is calculated what his power of *originality* may be, and therefore initiation, as soon as it embraces it, move him to just faith, and emancipate and *thaw his nature*.—I read about Indians" (Martí, 211). Thus, the Indian is definitely a natural man waiting to be thawed. We can, then, consider that the "natural Man" for Martí is both the Indian and the mestizo—white and Indian—as both have formed a close relationship with nature and, therefore, are able to bear the qualities of being *indigenous*, *legitimate*, and *original*, as well as carry the characteristic of being, for that reason, *subordinate subjects*. However, participation in an agrarian economy, and not only possession of real indigenous culture, seems to be, in the end, an important index in the definition of the natural man or woman. As he passes through Livingston, Martí refers to the "black as a *pure race*" that "brighten the eyes," and says this is a group that speaks "their *primitive* Caribbean, their *pure* dialect: they have not mixed it [he says] with Spanish words for Spanish innovations. Or they have invented their words, or they had them, which accuses *natural* wealth" (Martí, C.E., 48). Thus, *primitive*, *pure*, and *natural* are adjectives related to the character of the culture of the Black Caribbean in Livingston—compelled by the circumstance to transplant their culture, but without denying it—although it is not yet explicitly described as "natural man." At the height of 1893, in a profile dedicated to Generalissimo, generally speaking—without distinction of race or ethnic origin—Martí writes of "the natural men who came to war" (Martí, 446); and, in 1894, referencing the Caribbean's involvement in the independence plans in a letter to Gomez, he again qualifies them: "Blessed are all natural men, unique to whom one must expect something noble in this world!" (Martí, 340). But already since 1880, in a reading at a meeting of immigrants in Steck Hall, New York, he had included blacks and mulattos—mestizos in black and white—in that category of *natural*, leaning on their character as carriers of a legitimate identity and as factors of resistance in the culture imposed by the metropolitan power:

> Are men of color, blacks and mulattos,—because the mystery of a man should not be made like all others *natural* and simple.—Are they are perhaps the meek herd that obeyed the shepherd's interested hand, and the son of the elegiac marimba, the unique consolation forbidden at times I waited in calm time for a distant redemption? (Martí, 202)

Thus, the concept we are dealing with is subject to multiple variables. It is not definitively fixed, but we can gather that the natural man and woman are those who live in harmony with their circumstance—not linked to the city centers where the new patterns of modern capitalist culture are; where other things have violated the traditional patterns with more violence—and therein lies their authenticity and strength.

Martí's appreciation of the value for humanity of knowing and being able to achieve proper consonance with the natural environment in pursuit of nonaggressive development and well-being—and his insistence on pointing it out throughout his mature work—identifies Martí's early appreciation for man's part in the ecological system. Likewise, Martí demonstrates an understanding of the permanent adaptation of some societies to the environment or as agents of alterations, favorable or not, to that environment. Martí, from the Americas—in the decade following these Central American experiences and having already a more defined idea of the phenomenon—would say that human engagement in nature accelerates, changes, or stops this process of non-aggressive development and the pursuit of well-being.

I understand that great problems come as a result of first-world economies emphasizing capitalist development, which, by altering the traditional relationship of man with his resources—that is, the natural harmony that he advocates—negatively influenced the future of the particular cultures. Martí remarks on this, tangentially, when referring in Livingston to the scarcity of corn and to the abundance of cane:

> From this they live; the coconut, the yucca, the banana. [very limited subsistence agriculture wise] [American] corn is scarce, and cane [introduced according to commercial agriculture] abounds. (Martí, 38)

Scholar Pedro Pablo Rodríguez, on the other hand, clearly warns that "since his Mexican days Martí was a supporter of productive diversification"

(Rodriguez, 212–13). Rodríguez notes in his brochure *Guatemala*, of 1878, that he "saw with favorable eyes the expansion of the cultivation of coffee in that country," and he refers to "the need to increase the stockbreeding and to continue developing other crops and the exploitation forestry, so as not to make the single-pivot coffee of the nation's economy" (Rodriguez, 212–13). While this pragmatic concern is evident, there is, at the same time, a certain disappointment over the abandonment of traditional crops. Readers can deduce this indirectly by considering the evident pleasure which he extends in describing those environments where the natural culture has been respected and, therefore, where the ecological environment turns its back to the demands of the capitalist market:

> In Zacapa they live mainly on tobacco and straw hats: this is the *patrimony*, as the townspeople say. Trade, almost imperceptible to the foreigner; not easily seen, it is, however, active. Here they come from all the nearby valleys, to supply themselves with all kinds of necessities.—So almost all the houses of the people have sugar, liquors, fabrics, iron, earthenware, and the primitive articles indispensable for the life of the fields. (Martí, 44)

Sometimes Martí's discomfort in the face of altered natural environments becomes quite explicit:

> It is Earth, however, miserable; his children have not been able to exploit such rare advantages, such productive soil, so friendly a climate, and, without trade, without even traffic, without stimulus, without necessities, without employment, the rickety population diminishes, and the natives of the country, which in it have reached advanced age, they *emigrate*.—The Island of Women, endowed with the best bay, is at least sure that there will not be a thirsty traveler who will gladly contemplate how the Indian armed with a knife climbs up the slippery coconut tree its heavy and well stocked green cluster. (Martí, 32)

From this moment, there is a rejection of the alleged opposition between civilization and barbarism—artificial nature, domesticated nature *versus* original wild nature, which in some cases is concretized in the equivalent city-field opposition, by the thinking of those intent on imposing a modern civilization that was alien in the image and interest of European countries and the United States. Martí's most complete ideas on this can be found in "Our America" but, from his Central American backdrop, he presents almost an ironic contrast:

> Death is not possible here, among such gentle women, transparent waves, rumor of coconut palms and pure sky. While death is more natural, it is more beautiful. Solitary death is awesome; urban death, it's ridiculous. (Martí, 30)

In *Central America and the Disorders of the Republics of Central America*—texts referring to a journey of 1878 and which were, apparently, drafted in 1882[7]—Martí already presents a more scientific approach to the subject of the man-nature relationship, relying upon the growing development of modern natural science and technology:

> By force sweat, the country revives. Nature, tired of its laziness, works in a hurry. These people wake up, falling, rising painfully, like those who have slept too much;—but once awake, they want, putting their hands to work, avenging that shame of having slept while everyone was working. And as it is a land where there is nothing more to break with the plow to see the fruits sprout—it is beautiful to see how this country returns to life,—and its formerly lonely ways, are full of people coming and going; And its mountains hear cracked the [foete of Mulero], and its ports see numerous fruits come and go.[8]
>
> These republics will end up being no more than one, as the laws of nature, politics, and utility order it.[9]

This has also deepened his reflection on *A Trip to Venezuela*, of 1881, when he refers to the possible regeneration of the natural world:

> We arrived from Venezuela, still amazed at the sight of so many masterpieces of nature, hopeful again to see the generous efforts made by the country to repopulate their forests, renew their cities, accredit their ports and open their rivers to the world. (Martí, C.E., T. 11)

He also observes the need for diversification of crops:

> Venezuela is a rich country beyond natural boundaries. The mountains have gold, silver, and iron veins. The earth, which if it were a maiden, awakens at the slightest look of love. The Agricultural Society of France has just published a book showing that there is no country on Earth so well-endowed to establish in it all kinds of crops. Potatoes and tobacco can be planted there:—tea, cocoa, and coffee; The oak grows next to the palm tree. It is even seen in the same thorn the Malabar jasmine and the Malmaison rose in the same basket with the pear and the banana.[10] (Martí, C.E., T. 11)

In the known fragments of his manuscript "The Diary of Izabal to Zacapa"—which is not simply a diary, but memories organized according to notes of travel that were written after his arrival in Zacapa—their minor tones, anger, and even moments of humor illuminate some of the conditions modern man ends up imposing on himself. This "soup kitchen" without pretensions, as he defines it (Martí, C.E., 52), dedicates a special attention to the peculiar use of language—to localisms, neologisms, and all kinds of ungeneralized denominations—and manifests in the common talk of peasants he finds. Most of the time Martí underlines them by writing, and he feels obliged to explain them in the manner of a glossary. To a large extent, they refer to the cultural apprehension of the ecosystem on the part of man. Here is a particular example:

> He kills cars, which they call here the pigs. . . . Speak of the manaca, a palm of superb leaves whose peduncles start from the earth. . . . On the way, Aniceto tells me that ranch does not mean here hacienda as in Mexico but country house. (Martí, C.E., 57)

He is interested in this "singular language" because it reveals the "spirit of these peoples": "Peoples of sober language [says], *those seed and root peoples*" (Martí, C.E., 76). The "natural" phenomena here contribute directly to the metaphors used by the writer.

If at the beginning of the "The Diary of Izabal to Zacapa" we could say that the strange look of the passing traveler still prevailed, we can appreciate subtly, and in this very text, how that narrator begins to feel involved. It is not enough to observe and describe; it is necessary to participate in the circumstances. In chapter VII, by criticizing a rich and petulant farmer, Martí explicitly recognizes his personal involvement in the places and communities he observes. In other words, he is not a passive, objective observer:

> And it is said that I who enjoy the pleasant and talkative trade of spirits, and observe the advancement of news and praise, and hear the grief to stubbornly seek the remedy, I frowned and found myself amiss among those brick walls, and under that tile roof, poorer by its rudeness than the miserable muddy and the dry [manaca] of the thick sideboard of Gualán. (Martí, C.E., 70–71)

It should be considered that Martí, at some point, calls this type of testimonial document "Autohistory," and considers this approach responsible for explaining not only the new reality with which he stumbles, but, singularly, "How it comes, being who I am" (Martí, 52). When the time has come, the boundaries between witness and external reality disappear. The information-collecting observer gradually becomes a participating observer. In chapter IX, Martí directly reproduces a dialogue where he himself intervenes:

> —"Is it a march?" He asks me, holding the stirrup, a young benevolent boy, who has risen with the dawn.
> —"I'm on the go," I answer with shaking hands. Be kind and honest. (Martí, C.E., 73)

And the narrative continues. It does not make any clarification as in previous opportunities. Even in the text, the unusual Cuban idioms are underlined: "Is it a march?" "I'm on the go." There is a tacit acceptance of this "new" reality and the witness's incorporation into it. This reflection takes us by the hand to refer, very quickly, to the different voices present in the text.

The traveler-witness, at times, gives words to characters from the described context, who will then intervene directly: with this, we achieve a much more objective orchestral vision of the observed reality, in addition to propitiating the rescue of the oral traditions of those human groups. We find a clear example at the beginning of chapter VI, where Martí presents, verbatim, his dialogue with the rich farmer, with whom he has made part of the way:

> —"Remember, sir!" My rooster was crushed, fully crushed, my lord; When the other one comes, it was a rooster of Cobán, a flowered animal, of what is of great, my lord; it gives a shove to the clubfoot, and remember that gave my rooster a cry, gave a return, without na'a of return of cat, and of a shot, of a shot alone, cracked it.
> —Ah, what a rooster!
> —But remember that a wind comes in, and was flipping to the fence of Chepillo, and when I came to raise, remember what a shame! He had been stabbed by the knife, my lord.
> "That was not to tied well, Mr. Catalino Mañar.
> No, my lord, I turned to him, and I was bound to tie him to my compadre. But remember! That I have in Santiago a chicken Jiro, and on Saturday I will bring the challenge with the white hen, because my chicken has eleven raises, my Lord, and with that all rooster a lesson. (Martí, C.E., 67–68)

Of course, the narrator does not aspire to abandon control, always leading, of course, to the fulfillment of his mission of legitimizing identity. Thus, he does not cease to express its own sense of cultural belonging as a compulsory reference:

> When it collects all its brilliance this figure, toasted and enthusiastic like that of our earth; when it stands whole, burly as a *Baracoan*, of correct face *like a Holguin citizen*, of old and fiery speech *like a Camagüey citizen* [and continues to describe a traveler]. (Martí, C.E., 69)

The writing self that creates these notations, in the end, assumes his own personal experiences together with those of the evoked set of references, all resulting from a cultural contact that he finds in his path. The author, who is becoming a critical witness, tries to function as an impartial intermediary. Martí aims to serve as mediator for the different voices of the people—for the social values, customs, and expectations that the different human groups carry—and tries to register them through that peculiar joint discourse, markedly dialogic, where the first narrative person can rotate among the characters he finds. It is structuring a voice of voices, which tries to be representative—and that results in the final version—where, necessarily, he incorporates his own prescriptions.

We can observe the peculiar inscription made by the traveler Martí when referring to the women, Indian or mestizo, in Central America: a typically subordinate subject, by reason of gender, class, and race. We must begin by recognizing that such a record led to a suggestive territory of conflict over other areas of his work—earlier or contemporaneous—where he usually proposed a different duty for female behaviors. This is particularly noticeable in relation to the scope of the generic female roles allocated by tradition that were established by cultural tendencies other than colonial Hispanic, the latter of absolute preponderance in Cuba, where the indigenous presence barely left traces and the Afrocuban voices still exist only on the margins of the canon.

In his writing, Martí gives us, preferably, images of those who at some point in his text "The Island of Women" had been called "Women of the Earth"—"kindly, endowed with extreme affability, natural intelligence and great tenderness" or also jovial and passionate (Martí, 30–31). They are middle-class or poor women who lived at a distance from power centers and are attached to traditional economies.

According to Martí, these "natural" women remained associated mostly in areas governed by the same parameters in force during the colony, linked to the specific cultural dynamics of each of their communities, but not limited to the family environment—to the exclusive private space—as city women would have been.

In this author's opinion, the descendants of Mayans or Latinos—that is, mestizo children of Mayans and Spaniards—were linked to a nonmonotheistic religion with the existence of powerful deities of both sexes, their vision of the world, and the canons of social behavior that must be less male-centered than perspectives held by the Christian religion and responsible for establishing strict prescriptions to Hispanic societies.[11] In any case, they were carriers of an identity that Martí was obviously interested in revalidating.

In "The Diary of Izabal to Zacapa," Martí openly criticizes the vanity that surrounds the life of the new urban bourgeois—who reproduce, uncritically, patterns of life of European capitals—and the provincial aspiration to imitate them that becomes especially uncomfortable when reflected in women. Martí tells his friends Fermín and Eusebio Valdés-Domínguez, for example, of the sacrifice he suffered when he let himself speak:

> For a little daughter of the landlady, who spent her infancies in Guatemala; who was raised half-child and half lady, and who would bite the dust for speaking at her time with some city gentleman. (Martí, C.E., 44)

Earlier, in "Island of Women," Martí aimed critically at this feminine "weakness":

> In a nearby hut, the housewife, in an embroidered blouse, highlights the carved red strip on the clean linen, points out a wooden piece where recorded in

> golden letters reads an English name, that suspended on the door of the only quarter of the house. (Martí, C.E., 33)

The classic Spanish sources, where the young man Martí had absorbed his ideas assiduously, were transporting the misogyny of ascetic thinkers, whose continence had to guarantee human improvement, and the Biblical perspective that fixed woman as sinners more exposed to the danger of the Augustinian lustfulness than men. Martí declared his preference for such thinking because he felt women remained linked mainly to the private space where they could fulfill perfectly their functions, removed from corrupting public spaces such the dances, for example. For him, the good woman to a great extent was born "for motherhood" (Martí, 301), and she had to be permanently "close to the desk of her husband or near with the cradle of her son" (Martí, 195). He was not alone in assigning to women the current morality of his time. However, toward the end of his life, in one of his last letters concerning his fondness for "his girls," Maria and Carmen Mantilla, daughters of Carmen Miyares, he notes that they should prepare themselves for the "virtuous and independent work" "to be equal or superior"[12] (Martí, *Campaign Diaries*, 365) to men and, therefore, to assume definitely their free will, being consistent with the enlightenment sources of thought and—why not to conclude it?—with the experience of having lived in the different countries, as described in "Our America."

Nevertheless, it is necessary to say that Martí's proposal of an image of the woman for a Spanish-American modern world, at the end of his days, was still a question of a contradictory conceptualization and an idea in progress.

But to return to Martí's Guatemalan period and his peculiar inscription of the women of the ground: the first vision of the woman in Livingston reveals enormous pleasure, on having been thinking about seeing the reality correspond to the boss from which one had come declaring support. Then he describes with undeniable pleasure from the same first paragraph:

> There, white linens move in the beach; on the roughly sloping road, more that they go down, they roll black points: those are the industrious mothers, who go to the shore of the sea to whiten their clothes. (Martí, C.E., 37)

However, Martí soon declares his perplexity—although still complimentary—before certain women who work shoulder to shoulder with their men, who have a voice and make work in their own environment. They are strong. Thus, he referred in Livingston:

> These Caribs of opulent breasts are the cultivators of the fields; men fishing and trading; women sow and do their job of mothers and wives. . . . They are

> admirable, this vivacity, this generosity, this fraternity, this cleaning. (Martí, C.E., 38–39)

Martí recognizes a selfless generosity in these women, which complies with female stereotypes, but he also finds with ease "the soft, the delicate" which, together with the beauty, is how he could appreciate them more (Martí, 333). He writes a sentence, for example, describing the hostess Teosia on her way through the Roblar, on the way from Izabal to Zacapa:

> That body, square and unwrapped, is so ugly that it seems angry; that body imprudent and impolite, has not lived, however, many years. If you are a woman, why aren't you beautiful? . . . Since it is not tempting, or beautiful, or friendly, it is not women. (Martí, C.E., 75)

A classic example of this type of attitude we would find in the portrait of Lola, the woman who leads pack mules—presumably Indian because she is called "Woman of Corn"—and whom he obviously detests. His physical and psychological descriptions start in chapter I of the "The Diary of Izabal to Zacapa," and are continued, on and on, throughout the text. This is only the beginning of the prejudices:

> Her profile is correct, the nose, the short mouth, well done forehead, the sharp beard . . . but all these perfections of the form, routed by the culture, become numerous ugliness by lack of spiritual transparency. . . . She strides, drinks water in all the rivers, eats *corn tortillas* without ceasing, helps to load and unload her husband. (Martí, C.E., 54)
>
> . . . Lola hauls and Moors; And he knows how to strap a beast with a cruelty that disgusts and astonishes. (Martí, C.E., 58)

Fascinated in contrast by the beauty of the young women in Livingston, Martí had not hesitated to describe them sensually:

> They are loquacious with the tongue, with their eyes, with their hips, with their hands. . . . If they said love, these women would burn. Oh! And as you wear that black. . . . A blue nightgown, leaves the arms and neck in the air, and below the knees, makes way for the skirt that hangs him from the waist. The one who doesn't wear the nightgown alone! (Martí, C.E., 38)

It happens, then, that what he praises in the young women, he criticizes in married women, so Lola says horrified:

> The breast, *poor modesty*! it jumps into the eyes with an abominable transparency, because it is barely covered by the shirt of the holidays, of the finest Indian, as light as lace and as tulle.—And Aniceto loves her: that is her Lola. (Martí, C.E., 45–46)

He warns with certainty—though not satisfied—that the absence of censorship by the mule driver responds to the existence of different moral dimensions in these human groups. Martí verified that in his daily life the Mayan descendants were involved in an agrarian economy that allowed the woman a relatively greater participation in the public space. They played a decisive role outside the strictly familiar context and linked to the production of the group. That is, he did not see them as circumscribed to the role of reproduction and the care of the home and of the children, although these duties remained part of their responsibility, so much so that in Livingston, where the beautiful, demonized women "burn"—very attuned to the modern erotic cliché of the "femme fatale"—he does not have to conclude: "It is a moral, pure, hardworking people" (Martí, C.E., 39).

It is necessary to clarify that this Lola not only contradicts but subverts his paradigm; she not only acts openly in the public space but lives the public space, in the midst of nature; she is an itinerant woman, homeless, working as a man, without children, and without modesty. So Martí's rejection of her, from his values we know, must be absolutely justified.

But progressively, even in his disgust, Martí, surprised by that pure and unbiased dialogue of the Indian or the black Garifuna with his surroundings, begins to understand; then Martí mocks himself and corrects his fierce preconceived criteria when, finally, the portrait of Teosia suddenly becomes a positive sign. She returns to his presence in "stretched shirt, fixed braid, and freshened face, and arrives abrupt, affectionate" (Martí, C.E., 39).

We must conclude, then, that Martí's discourse is committed, gradually, to recognize silenced female voices, which, although they contradict the paradigm that he had tried to fix until then in those texts that could be considered programmatic,[13] operate in a "natural," "canonical" way within their cultures. Arriving at this understanding, traveler-Martí stands as an intermediary: not only does he describe these women, not only does he try to reflect his behaviors, but he also proposes—in some cases directly and in others implicitly—to gather his reflections in the environment in which these people had to live. Necessarily, in the end, Martí feels an awareness of guilt before this series of absolute and so poorly founded judgments that he has been using. He recognizes it explicitly toward the end of the "The Diary of Izabal to Zacapa":

> How many individual events are subject to the strictest human justice! Sympathies and repugnance invisibly tilt the sentences. . . . With fear I write how much I write, and do what I do, because it possesses me, at the same as my blind spirit, unique, a parched distrust of myself, and I fear that, as I correct today yesterday's doubts, I must correct tomorrow which, abruptly and vehemently, I am stirring today. (Martí, C.E., 51)

To dwell on these nuances of Martí's particular descriptions of the subordinate Central American woman of the earth, as he passes through Central American territories, must serve to clarify an indissoluble relationship between people and the landscapes in which they live—"understood as a territorial system dialectically integrated by the natural components and derivatives of the modifying action of man" (Ramos, 239). In addition, it allows us to observe how, at the same time, a formative reflection of a conscious discourse of resistance toward "the other" was being established, before the expansion of industrial capitalism that threatened to change nature and man—that is, we see in Martí's writing our American culture produced the adaptation process of the "natural man" to his (or her) consubstantial ecological habitat.

NOTES

1. This chapter was originally published in *ILE, Yearbook of Ecology, Culture and Society*. No. 3, Year 3 of 2003.

2. Pedro Pablo Rodríguez in his "Guatemala: José Martí on the Way to Our America" (*Yearbook of the Center of Martíanos Studies*, Havana No. 17, Center for Martíanos Studies, 1994) provides enlightening historical elements and political nuances around this discovery and the genesis of Martí's fascination with the Latin American continent.

3. Notwithstanding his obvious overcoming of the limited habits, at times and throughout his travel literature, Martí continues to use romantic descriptive influences: "An impetuosity, mixed continuously with poetic reflections," such as Callejas and Álvarez have admired since Martí's first testimony (the political imprisonment in Cuba), and influenced by the prose of Víctor Hugo (Bernardo Callejas); Luis Álvarez: "The Testimony and the Chronicles in Martí until 1880," in the *Yearbook of the Center of Studies Martianos*, Havana No. 17, 1994, p. 275. Regarding the nationalism vogue, we must not forget that need to reaffirm the same against European culture when it was concretized among us, especially in the then, very popular "picturess of customs" widely circulated by the press of the time and that Martí must have known very well. Carmen Suárez in her *José Martí and Víctor Hugo in the Faithful of the Modernity* (Havana, Center for Research and Development of Cuban culture Juan Marinello-Editorial José Martí, 1997) refers, precisely, to that which José Agustín Caballero, Varela and Luz and Caballero demanded for Cuba: a similar literature, a recognition of customs, and a historical and social analysis of the reality. This was an urgency that Martí would extend to the countries he visited

4. Part of my analysis was around the conceptualizations of the collective identities expressed, fundamentally, in the texts of Carolina de la Torre: "Conscience of Sameness: Cuban Identity and Culture" (*Topics and Identities* No. 2, April–June, 1995) (Havana, Center for Research and Development of Cuban Culture "Juan Marinello," 2001; Cintio Vitier ("Cuba: Its Latin American and Caribbean Identity," text read in the Latin American and Caribbean chair, at the Centre for Martíanos Studies, March 25, 1992); Enrique Ubieta Gómez (*Essays of Identity*, City of Havana, Editorial Cuban Letters, 1993); and Armando Cristóbal ("Precisions on Nation and Identity," in *Topics* No. 2, April–June, 1995.)

5. I use the term "real" because, to a great extent, the new independent Hispanic states lived a long postcolonial period during which the lives of these peoples were little varied. Martí himself would declare in his "New Codes," conceived after the Mexican experience and his first tour of Central America: "The independence, proclaimed with the help of the Spanish authorities, was no more than nominal—and did not penetrate the popular layers . . . : Only the form was altered" (*José Martí: Complete Works*, T. 19, ed. cit., p. 96). And more he said, "We governed our original times with laws of the expired ages" (*José Martí: Complete Works*.

Critical Edition, T. 5, ed. cit., pp 89–90). The Guatemalan experience, above all, gave rise to these considerations. We know that, after three centuries of metropolitan power, the beginnings of Guatemala's postcolonial period were notoriously irregular. It had proclaimed its independence on September 16, 1821, and almost immediately, in 1822, Agustín de Iturbide—who had been crowned Emperor as Agustín I by the Viceroy Juan O'Donojú—incorporated Central America into the Mexican Empire, acting against the desires of the majority of the population. Guatemala did not recover its autonomy, really, until 1823, when a liberal revolution in Mexico forced Iturbide to abdicate. The Federation of the United Provinces of Central America was then established, comprised of the current republics of Guatemala, Honduras, El Salvador, Nicaragua, and Costa Rica, which remained definitively dissolved in 1842. Since then, three decades had elapsed at the arrival of Martí.

6. It would be convenient, too, to remember that, already in 1882, Martí would write in his "Notebooks of Notes": "For me, the word Universe explains the Universe: *Versus uni*: I vary it in the one" (Martí, José, *Complete Works*, t. 21, ed. cit., p. 255), signifying a characteristic mode of man's relationship with his natural environment: nature is not seen as subordinate, and man ceases to be its center and end absolute. Such a sense of harmonious uniqueness that could assist him, then, can be seen as a result of a maturation of those contemporary ideas that influenced his thought; for example, Emerson's romantic transcendentalism and natural harmony invoked by Whitman. Whitman's works evidenced the need for conservation of nature for the survival of civilization.

7. Originally known as "L'Ámerique Centrale" y "Les Troubles des Républiques de L'Ámérique Centrale."

8. Martí, José: "Central America" (unpublished translation), *Complete Works*. Critical Edition, T. 11 (in editorial process), Havana, Center for Martíanos Studies.

9. Martí, José: "The disorders of the republics of Central America . . . " (Unpublished translation), *Complete Works*. Critical edition, T. 11 (in editorial process), ed. cit.

10. Martí, José: A Trip to Venezuela" (unpublished translation), *Complete Works*. Critical Edition, T. 11 (in editorial process, ed. cit.)

11. The Maya conceived an explanation for the birth of the world, very close to what Christianity provides in the biblical book of Genesis, in which a couple, a man and a woman—the Grandfather (the Creator) and the Grandmother (the Formmaker)—decided to generate life. After several attempts, they finally succeeded in making human beings from corn grains—the "Men of Corn." There were exactly four men, and, from their bodies, they gave birth to four women who, in this way, and as it happened in the book of Genesis, were dependent on men since their birth. Also from this came the most powerful male figure in the Mayan pantheon known as Itzamná, Lord of Fire and of the heart, which is linked with the Man God of the Sun. There is also the powerful goddess woman of the Moon, Ixchel, the deity of the feminine arts, represented as an old woman, bad tempered and demonized. Ixchel is, in addition, the protector of the births. We also have, in the bible of the Mayan, demon and procreation states—evil and sex—linked to the figure of the woman. However, according to some myths, it is one of the four split personalities of Itzamná: of course, the most perverse. Martí, surely, should already know through his encyclopedic reading at least some general aspects of the Mayan-Quiché culture, although we do not have previous or contemporary evidence in his work. However, obviously during his trip to Merida and Chichen Itza before his departure for Progreso, he was put in direct contact with cultural Mayan referents, which should be well enlightening. His encounter and the dialogs which held true in *Isla Mujeres* with British archaeologist Augustus Le Plongeon—Browser of Mayan ruins of the Yucatan Peninsula—were surely even more illustrative. We find the earliest reference of these experiences, and to information he will compile on the issue in his written work in the height of 1878, in his pamphlet *Guatemala*, published in Mexico, just one year after having made his annotations of "Livingston" and its "Diary of Izabal to Zacapa." In *Guatemala* he speaks of José Milla, who writes with notorious scholarship and who studies "the times in which princesses fought kachiques, quiches, and zutujiles" (*José Martí: Complete Works*. Critical Edition, T. 5, ed. cit., p. 273). Martí denounces Milla's probable knowledge of the ancient history of Central America, subsequently, in 1884, devoting a comment from the pages of *La América*. There he would mention, explicitly, the story Mayan of Genesis that the historian reproduces, that of the Popol Vuh. In 1888, in

his article "Guatemala, the Land of the Quetzal," published in *The American Economist*, Martí speaks about "the Popol Vuh," translated by Brasseur and Ximenes, and Milla, who used this history to narrate in faithful verses the picturesque creation of the Quiché Bible (*Jose Martí: Complete Works*, t. 7, ed. cit., p. 183). This example testifies to Martí's knowledge of the Spanish version of the Popul Vuh, by Francisco Jiménez—under the title of *Book of the Community*—and the French edition by Brasseur de Bourbourg.

12. José Martí: *Campaign Diaries*, ed. Crit. Mayra Beatriz Martínez and Froilán Escobar, Havana, Casa Editora Abril, 1996, p. 365.

13. Among the texts that can be considered to have programmatic intentions with regard to the topic that occupies us, prior to 1877, and whose proposal of paradigm of female behavior to a certain extent—directly or indirectly—contrasts with that recorded in these travel annotations, we must consider, first of all, his work *Adulteress*, in his first version of 1874. The constant reflections of censorship his two characters execute—symptomatically, male—are directed to the disqualified character of the infidel, who seeks satisfaction out of wedlock. Among the female figures, only the mother who is faithful to her subordinate role as protector of the home is saved from the phallic condemnation. This is how Grossermann, the leading character, expresses his preeminence to his wife: "For me, for me only your whole soul, your life before, your life now, your minor thoughts, all your lives.—truth, the light of mine, that everything is for me?" (*José Martí: Complete Works*, t. 18, ed. cit., p. 39). The bulletins published in the Magazine Universal in 1875 express clearly Martí's ideas about the passive role and strict support for men that is attributed to women, among other reasons, by the weaknesses that are considered inherent: Number 3, May—"Heroes are born, but women, a creature of tenderness, do not have this vigorous and active mission in this life of the earth" (*Jose Martí: Complete Works*. Critical Edition, t. 2, ed. cit., 2000, p. 41); number 4, August—"Tramp and without purpose a living being walks . . . if you do not have . . . for his forehead sweaty and wound, asylum in some breast of women" (Ibid., p. 163). Also, "Friendship is as beautiful as love: it is love itself, devoid of the charming women" (Ibid., p. 165). In addition, we find contradictory assertions to his travel texts of '77, in his proverb love with love is paid (1875). There the leading male character refers to the virtues appreciated in each sex: "In him, courage and tenderness, / In her, discrete grace" (*José Martí: Complete Works*, t. 18, ed. cit., p. 115). The female protagonist, in correspondence to the paradigm, reaffirms it: "¡Wait, wait, my love: / Stop your promises/ Timidities of women/ That the value of love increases!" (Ibid., p. 124)—how alien this feminine image to our Lola! Another moment that ratifies the model of women dedicated to work, preferably in the protected space of family, is in the newsletter published in March 1876, "The Masonic Feast," where Martí defends the possibility of women's access to a public event on the basis that it will no longer be restricted by the men to whom it is "naturally" attached: "this access is a victory for women, who are no longer reluctant to attend a place where they know that their husbands, sons, and brothers will be and do not struggle in any way with their morality or honesty." In any case, a change of position begins to be observed here, with what he notices happens inevitably in life (*Jose Martí: Complete Works*. Critical Edition, t. 2, 2000, ed. cit., p. 269. The highlight, in all cases is the author).

WORKS CITED

Center for Research and Development of Cuban Culture "Juan Marinello," 2001.

Cristóbal, Armando. "Precisions on Nation and Identity." *Topics* No. 2, April–June, 1995.

Gómez, Enrique Ubieta. *Essays of Identity*. City of Havana. Editorial Cuban Letters, 1993.

Martí, José. *Campaign Diaries*, ed. Crit. Mayra Beatriz Martínez and Froilán Escobar, Havana, Casa Editora Abril, 1996.

Martí, José. *Complete Works*, Social Sciences Publishing House, Havana 1975.

José Martí: Complete Works. Critical Edition, T. 5. Havana, Center for Martíanos Studies, 2001.

Mateo, José M. "The Culture of Nature as a Basis for Environmental Education." *Ilé*, no. I, 2001.

Ramos, Maria del Carmen Víctori, et al. "Landscape, Traditional Discourse and Family in Shaping the Cultural Regions in Cuba." *Thoughts and Popular Traditions*. Center for Research and Development of Cuban culture "Juan Marinello," 2000.

Rodríguez, Pedro Pablo. "Guatemala: José Martí on the Way to Our America." *Yearbook of The Center of Martíanos Studies*, Havana No. 17. Center for Martíanos Studies, 1994.

de la Torre, Carolina. "Conscience of Sameness: Cuban Identity and Culture." *Topics and Identities* No. 2, April–June, 1995.

Vitier, Cintio. "Cuba: Its Latin American and Caribbean Identity." Text read in the Latin American and Caribbean chair, at the Centre for Martíanos Studies.

Chapter Four

Antonio Nuñez Jiménez, Oswaldo Guayasamín, and the Recovery of Cuba's Progressive Intellectuals

Susan Bender

Antonio Nuñez Jiménez. I had never heard his name, or been aware of his role in the formation of modern Cuba, before arriving at the Antonio Nuñez Jiménez Foundation for Man and Nature [Fundacion Antonio Nuñez Jiménez de la Naturaleza y el Hombre] in Havana at the beginning of December 2016. I was stunned by the breadth and depth of the life work of Antonio Nuñez Jiménez, who played many key roles in Cuba before, during, and after the revolution from 1953 to 1959 and in the ensuing years. Indeed, he was part of the core group of leaders working with Fidel Castro, with particular responsibility for coordinating the agricultural reform of Cuba after the revolution and during much of the half-century U.S. embargo when the nation needed to become self-sufficient. Agricultural reform in Cuba meant, as he uniquely understood, developing sustainable practices that would protect the natural environment.

In recognition of Nuñez Jiménez's important contributions to Cuban society, the Antonio Nuñez Jiménez Foundation was established in 1994 and is "dedicated to the research and promotion of culturally and socially directed environmental protection" ("Alternatives"). The vision of the Foundation reads: "A Cuban society with a developed environmental conscience that will recognize nature as part of its identity, and an active institution in the development of environmental and cultural values in Cuba and the world" ("Strategic Document"). The mission of the Foundation is: "To work towards a culture of nature, with the objective of creating harmony between society and its environment" ("Strategic Document"). Among the many important achievements and activities Nuñez Jiménez was involved with during his life, his work as an environmentalist and as someone who appreciated the intersections between human culture and the more-than-human world particularly stood out and have become the focus of the foundation that now exists and bears his name.

I joined a group of environmentally oriented professors and writers from the United States who traveled to Cuba to participate in a two-day academic environmental symposium held at the foundation. We were ushered into high-ceilinged rooms lined with bookcases containing a vast collection of Nuñez Jiménez's life work—research notes, manuscripts, and publications. Nuñez Jiménez lived from April 20, 1923, to September 13, 1998. He was an archeologist, geographer, naturalist, academic, and revolutionary; he served as captain of the revolutionary forces of Che Guevara and later as Minister of Agrarian Reform in Cuba. It was clear that he was a prolific scholar with a range of interests and an impressive body of work, now housed at the foundation, which is managed by his daughter, Liliana Nuñez, who serves as the president of the foundation.

Although Nuñez Jiménez was a polyglot and a hands-on adventurer who explored much of South America and the Caribbean, collecting cultural artifacts and natural specimens, he was also particularly notable as a scholar who wrote about the intersections between nature and human society. In her 2007 volume *La esperanza del mundo: La edad de oro y la construcción de una ética y una cultura ambiental* [The Hope of the World: The Golden Age and the Construction of an Ethical and Environmental Culture], Mariana G. Serra García cites Nuñez Jiménez's notable contribution to the concept of a fundamental unity between humans and nature, especially in his 2002 posthumous publication *José Martí: la naturaleza y el hombre* [José Martí: Nature and Humanity]. She quotes Armando Hart from the book's forward: "Esta selección de textos martianos y lost análisis de Nuñez Jiménez me recuerdan que para el genuine intellectual cubano los studios de la Naturaleza en sus relaciones con el Hombre constituyen premisas essenciales para la ciencia, la cultura y la política prática" (García, 24). Nuñez Jiménez's magnum opus as an environmental writer and scholar may be his 1998 book *Hacia una cultura de la naturaleza* [Making a Culture of Nature], which opens with an epigraph from Martí, the Cuban poet, writer, and political leader, who died in 1895. The epigraph, which reads "Estudiar las fuerzas de la Naturaleza y aprendar a manejarlas es la manera más derecha de resolver los problemas sociales," suggests that we might best solve society's problems by studying the forces of the natural world. This is a resounding statement of support for natural science and for the concept that there is an essential unity between nature and society.

During the December 2016 symposium in Havana, in between listening to the papers and readings by Cuban and American writers, I found myself drawn in by many of the paintings on the walls of the foundation—large, stark, intense, colorful—several of Antonio Nuñez Jiménez, but also paintings of his wife, Lupe Velis, and of course Fidel Castro. The paintings were signed by an artist named "Guayasamín." I was intrigued by the images, but I had not heard of this painter before.

Back in the United States, I learned from the internet that Oswaldo Guayasamín (July 6, 1919–March 10, 1999) was an Ecuadorian master painter and sculptor of Quechua and Mestizo heritage who was born in Quito. Guayasamín's best friend died during a demonstration in Quito while Guayasamín was a student in college; this experience inspired the painting "Los Niños Muertos" (The Dead Children) and had a profound impact on the artist's vision of human nature and society. Thereafter he focused his work on themes of injustice, oppression, poverty, and human suffering.

Guayasamín was "a passionate supporter of the communist Cuban Revolution and Fidel Castro" ("Oswaldo," *Widewalls*). He traveled to many countries throughout Latin America during his life, observing indigenous people and taking note of poverty and hunger, which he poignantly represented through visual art. The paintings in the Antonio Nuñez Jiménez Foundation indicate that he visited Cuba at various points in history and had a relationship with Antonio Nuñez Jiménez, as well as Fidel Castro. The walls displayed several paintings of Antonio, made at different times throughout their relationship.

Guayasamín was recognized by the U.N. Educational, Scientific and Cultural Organization and given a prize for his dedication to "an entire life of work for peace." He is considered a national treasure in Ecuador, and after his death in 2002, La Capilla del Hombre ("The Chapel of Man") opened, containing many of his paintings and sculptures depicting man's cruelty to man. He intended this space also to be a tribute to the achievements of the Latin American people, from the pre-Columbian world through the era of conquest and colonization and up to the present. La Capilla del Hombre is located in Guayasamín's former home in the hills above Quito ("Oswaldo," *Guayasamín*).

Though venerated in his home country and in Cuba, Guayasamín was criticized by the U.S. government when he painted a mural of the history of Ecuador in 1988; the mural included a male figure wearing a Nazi helmet with "CIA" lettering on it. According to the Cubans, Che Guevara was captured and murdered with the assistance of the Central Intelligence Agency while traveling in Bolivia in 1967. Many in Cuba and other parts of Latin America viewed the U.S. government's activities, often performed by the CIA, as a violent colonial intrusion into the affairs of sovereign nations in the hemisphere. Learning about Guayasamín's life and political views led me to wonder whether the anti-American streak in his work is one of the reasons for the apparent neglect of his art in American academic and popular circles. In the United States, we have certainly learned a lot about the activists and politicians who led the Cuban revolution, but the intellectuals and artists who supported them seem to have faded into the background.

What was the connection between Guayasamin and Cuba's leaders? The Revolutionaries, and in particular Che Guevara, are credited with orchestrating the agrarian reform, initiating the Cuban Literacy Campaign, and promoting open education in which "The University must paint itself black, mulatto, worker, and peasant." As a medical doctor, Che focused on universal health care and medical education; he played an important role in making this a priority in Cuba. As a young medical student, Che traveled throughout Latin America and became radicalized by the poverty, hunger, and disease he witnessed. It seems to have been this overarching concern for the poor, oppressed, and suffering that resonated with Guayasamín and drew him to Cuba's leaders, including Antonio Nuñez Jiménez.

As a political scientist and interculturalist, I was interested to learn more about the Cuban perspective of the Revolution as well as the more recent history of Cuban-American relations. I expected to find a great deal of anger toward the United States, given the six decades of anti-Cuban policies promoted by the U.S. government. Our entourage of environmental writers and

Figure 4.1. Foundation Library with Guayasamín paintings on the wall. Photograph by Susan Bender

Figure 4.2. Entrance to the Antonio Nuñez Jiménez Foundation, Havana, Cuba. Photograph by Susan Bender

scholars had arrived in Havana the day after the official national week of mourning following the death of Fidel Castro. Obviously, there was a great deal of celebration and discussion of his accomplishments during this time, and many pictures and flowers were on display throughout the city. During a tour of Old Havana, our guide, Luis, talked about the Cuban reality "before" the revolution. The city had been controlled by the mafia, Luis said, who in turn, controlled the police through bribery and corruption. The mafia imported and promoted drug abuse, alcohol, gambling, and prostitution. Others talked of U.S. corporations that controlled land and resources, exploiting the Cuban peasants. It seemed to many Cubans that they had little control of their country and there was no rule of law. There had been a tremendous gap between the wealthy few—many of whom were not even Cuban—and the majority of Cubans who suffered under a corrupt political and social reality.

It was a privilege to visit Havana for this symposium on environmental literature and to experience, if only for a few days, this amazing place and its people; and to wonder, through the paintings of Oswaldo Guayasamín, about the progressive vision of Cuban intellectuals and political leaders such as Che Guevara and Fidel Castro as well as figures like Antonio Nuñez Jiménez, whose names less frequently appear in the American media. Guayasamín's impressionistic renderings of prominent Cubans imply nuance and complexity, far from the simplified caricatures we typically receive in the United States. His particular devotion to Nuñez Jiménez as a contemplative, multifaceted scholar, helps to elevate this twentieth-century Cuban, so seldom mentioned in American scholarly circles, to the status of a latter-day Alexander von Humboldt.

WORKS CITED

"Antonio Nuñez Jiménez, Che Guevara's Comrade, 75." https://www.nytimes.com/1998/09/16/us/antonio-nunes-jimenez-che-guevara-s-comrade-75.html. September 16, 1998. Retrieved January 3, 2019.

Antonio Nuñez Jiménez Foundation for Man and Nature [Fundacion Antonio Nuñez Jiménez de la Naturaleza y el Hombre]. Alternatives: Solidarity in Action. https://www.alternatives.ca/en/allies/antonio-jimenez-foundation-man-and-nature-cuba

Nuñez Jiménez, Antonio. *Hacia una cultura de la natureleza*. Editorial Si-Mar S.A., 1998.

———. *José Martí: la naturaleza y el hombre*. Fundacíon Antonio Nuñez Jiménez de la Naturaleza y el Hombre, 2002.

"Oswaldo Guayasamín." *Widewalls*. https://www.widewalls.ch/artist/oswaldo-guayasamin/. May 7, 2013. Retrieved January 3, 2019.

"Oswaldo Guayasamín." *Guayasamín*. http://guayasamin.org/index.php/oswaldo-guayasamin/biografia. Retrieved January 3, 2019.

Serra García, Mariana G. *La esperanza del mundo: La edad de oro y la constuccion de una ética y una cultura ambiental*. Publicaciones Acuario, 2007.

"Strategic Document for the Urban Sustainability Program." City Farmer, Canada's Office of Urban Agriculture. http://www.cityfarmer.org/NunezUA.html

Chapter Five

Lydia Cabrera and the Narrative of Nature

Margarita Mateo Palmer,
Translated by Stephanie Thom

According to María Zambrano, Lydia Cabrera begins *Black Stories of Cuba* (1940) by sharing her approach with nature, one of the fundamental pillars of her stories. Part of her island [Cuba] can be seen as the birthplace of gods and mythologies, and also as home to an inextinguishable metamorphosis. Cabrera later explains in her great work *The Mountain*, the Bible of Cuban Santeria, that the animation of natural forces is one of the fundamental principles of the Afro-Cuban religions, which in turn, has left a strong imprint on the imaginary and national culture. But it is one thing to believe in the spirituality of the mountain, and another to create a narrative work where nature has become a primary element, such that it can be considered a leading character based on the rules of narratology.

In very different ways—and various textual levels—natural elements are integral to the stories of the first book published by Lydia Cabrera. The most notable aspect is the presence of animals. Not only do they play important active roles, but they also become main characters in the narrative, a common practice throughout history, such as in myths and ancient fables. However, in Cuban works animals acquire very peculiar features.

Mrs. Hicotea, Godfather Horse, Taita Tiger, and Man Chivo are some of the original animal characters in this Cuban narrative tradition; they are not only indigenous, but also African. The anthropomorphizing of the animals happens in different ways. Mrs. Hicotea, for example, can appear reading *Illustrated Havana* on the banks of a creek; the wife of Taita Tiger sits down in her house to play the piano; the frog, which when the world was young had hair, makes cigarettes. These characters are some of the forms, pleasant and ingenious. We see, for instance, how a cow dresses up formally as if to issue a royal edict: "it put on satin yellow shoes and wore an outfit of celestial blue muslin with extensive embroidered strips. . . . He made his way to the village mounted on a mule" (93).[1] The reader associates the animal characters with human features, and even the narrator refers to them as male or female. Unexpected details appear to remind readers of the characters' animal identities. For example, Taita, turtle, and deer, known as the "Leg of Air," are already prosperous farmers on the happy island when they arrived in 1845—one of them has a hut and a saddled pony. They argue heatedly. Turtle suddenly extends "his neck black and yellow striped" (78) in a gesture that foregrounds its animal form; a few lines later, it appears with "rolled-up pants that were always too wide" (79).

In this game of representations, identities of the characters become mobile, open, and changing, adopting forms of fluidity, which defy any reduction or consolidation of their features. The differences between obvious expressions of the natural world are usually deleted, even if unique qualities suddenly appear that force the reader to avoid a convenient classification of the characters, but these qualities add to the constant mobility of the notions behind the animal characters. A clear example of this confusion between the human and the animal—a dilution of frontiers which contributes to the dynamism of the observable world—is accomplished with "Bregantino, Bregantín." In this long story, composed of three narratives developed separately, the Queen of Cocozumba, a black woman who smokes tobacco, argues with the King who is lying in his hammock on the plantation to escape the heat of that summer day. The King wants to marry their daughter to a healthy and robust man with good qualities, and the Queen scolds her spouse, emphasizing the daughter's human condition and her difference from a species considered inferior. "As if the girl was a beast, a dog in heat . . . without education!" (15) she blurts out at the King in a way that this gives greater importance to the marriage. However, immediately after that, the Queen brags about her ancestors and reminds him that they are descended from the first Elephant that lived in the forest, in a boast of their animal lineage which contradicts his earlier rejection.

In this way the identity of Lombriz is formed—a character created entirely by Lydia Cabrera, not rewritten from the mythological accounts, as argued by some scholars. Its description can be seen with greater clarity than other characters. Lombriz, an earthworm, is determined the winner of a test and will be permitted to marry the princess. Since the beginning of the story, it has become clear that the worm "was not a worthless worm, nor more disgusting than some men" (19). The King becomes angry in the presence of the weak Lombriz, who can be hesitant, an expression of coy sadness, a cloying look of sickly melancholy, colorless and skinny, sometimes soft and other times tense (23).

In the third year of the celebrated marriage, Lombriz feels his health decline. He loses sight and rejects the sunlight; the air makes him sneeze; he has a fever; and he decides to leave the surface of the Earth forever (21). Of this decision, Lombriz tells his servant the Bull, "If there ever was a time when you felt the need to wish to see your former owner, dig the Earth with your hoof. . . . Earthworm can give you advice or an example. Or find me in yourself" (22). "Find me in yourself" alludes to worms' parasitic condition in the intestines of other living beings; this leaves no doubt of the "worminess" of the character that will finally disappear into "the hole of any drain, reducing size, and taking the shape that today is known and avoided" (23). At this point the third-person narrator describes in detail the physical traits that worm had possessed until then: "before he had been a white man, tiny factions, thin lips, bitter, a little mustache; bald, bulky chested, short legs and arms, so short, that made him seem like he was always sitting although he was standing, steep, and as though corseted and permanently afflicted" (23–24). María Zambrano alludes to this peculiar treatment of the character and its transformation from human to animal in her work "Lydia Cabrera, Poet of the Metamorphosis," stating that "things and beings, are determined and fixed, and are imprisoned in an appearance always the same" (130). Zambrano notes that, for Cabrera, order and security of the world was extremely reassuring, composed of things equal to themselves and distributed in families, species, and genera. For humans, it is as if a subtle layer of ash was spread over the radiance of the glory of the world, of the array of life, ungraspable and in perpetual metamorphosis (130).

Defending the laws of nature, a respect established by tradition, is the focus of some stories, such as "Cheggue," in which a hunter who is in the Bush with his son warns him: "These days we are forbidden to hunt, because just as we celebrate the holidays of the year and have fun in the village, animals also celebrate their own holidays and have fun on the mountain" (43). One the first morning of the new year, however, Cheggue gets permission from his father to return to the mountain to collect his arrow, and to his surprise sees a large group of animals eating and drinking (44). He shoots an arrow and kills the oldest animal. The boy will pay with his life for committing this transgression, violating an established taboo meant to protect animals. Similarly, in "Bregantino Bregantín," the narrator notes the action of the young bull returning procreation in the Kingdom as follows: "And with this, nature again regained its rights, and boys were born in Cocozumba" (42).

The rural areas where the majority of the tales are set is considered to be privileged. Some stories, though, make references to elements of a city environment—churches, markets, streets with names and numbers, squares, and even neighborhoods or villages like Arroyo Naranjo or Yaguajay. These reference points allow the reader to locate certain stories in urban environments, but the undisputed *topos* of the tales is the mountain, that sacred space, a place of deep spirituality, the source of life and protection. As Lydia Cabrera states, the mountain contains essentially everything that the black person needs for his/her magic, for the preservation of health and well-being: everything one needs to defend oneself against any adverse force, by providing the elements of protection (9).

The believer's connection with the vegetation of the mountain, his dependence on the plants there, is also the basis of Lydia Cabrera's approach to nature: a living nature, where plants are endowed with powers. These witch's plants have a very particular relationship with the man. Likewise, the natural elements are frequently integrated into the metaphors, similes, and other tropes that are a fundamental part of her prose.

Nature, finally, is the fundamental source of the poetic language characteristic of this work, where the flora and fauna—fruits, meats, vegetables, Cuban trees, as well as the description of the landscape—play a major role. For example, the initial disorder of the world newly created by Abá Ogó blowing on his feces not only has the fluidity of the original cosmogonies, but is evident in the very language of the story: "Lacking a bit of order: fish peed in the flowers; the birds hung their nests in the crests of the waves. (The seas flowed from the snails; the rivers came from the tears of the first crocodile that had pity.) Mosquito sank his dart in the buttock of the mountain, and the entire mountain range was set in motion" (59–60).

Equally, the natural elements are often integrated into metaphors, similes, and other tropes which are a fundamental part of Cabrera's prose. For example:

- "The mangos, in which one drank warm, melted, the sun" (73);
- "The caimitos [fruit] sumptuous purple, the color of the lips of black people" (73);
- "[The] perfumed guanábanas [soursop], already hung by folding the branches with their weight, swollen and soft, like the breasts of pregnant women" (73);
- "One foot Osaín [an orisha]. . . . The bottom of the mountain, like an old tree, twisted, rough; the sonorous backs of insects buzzing; golden, dream of slow lizards" (242);
- "it opened, as a fan, the morning" (25);
- or "the funeral velvet wings" of the Tataguas, dark butterflies (66).

In sum, Cabrera exhalts nature and rejects some of the consequences of civilization, especially urbanization. Later, in *The Mountain*, she writes, "Without a doubt, cement, which condemns the living surface of the Earth to the death and silence, is the worst enemy of the wild African divinities. Urbanism, without civility or faith, alienates the orishas of the essence of Osaín, Oggún, Ochosi, 'who need the heat and the sap of the earth to thrive'" (63). Nature takes on a special meaning in the narratives of Lydia Cabrera; it constitutes a fundamental part of a literary discourse that, from its peculiar identification with the natural forces, its rejection of anthropocentrism, and its aesthetic complexity, remains to this day one of the most eloquent artistic expressions of Cuba's environment.

NOTE

1. The translation of Lydia Cabrera is original.

WORK CITED

Cabrera, Lydia. *Cuentos negros de Cuba* (Black Stories of Cuba). La Veronica, 1940.

Chapter Six

The Postcolonial Ecology of the New World Baroque

Alejo Carpentier's The Lost Steps

George B. Handley

In the late nineteenth and early twentieth centuries, primitivism was a widespread and vital artistic strategy of postcolonial resistance for Latin American writers. This essentially white and urban appeal to give representation to the nonwhite and rural populations of various Latin American nations marked a rhetorical turn to regional, local, and racial differences as signs of new Latin American cultural possibility in the wake of political independence. Of course, the rhetoric didn't always match the political reality, especially since much of Latin America's political changes in the early decades of the twentieth century failed to redress its persistent colonial structures. White patriarchal and paternalistic oligarchies continued to control land and political power, while millions of yeoman workers continued to work land they didn't own. These were largely indigenous and/or Afro-Latin American subjects, unlettered and with little or no social mobility. The majority of indigenist and other regionalist artists during this period of Latin American modernism were part of a white urban and lettered elite whose work often served the interests of national consolidation at the expense of those very peoples and places on the margins that their fiction sought to rescue. One thinks of the indigenism of Guatemala's Miguel Angel Asturias, the negritude of Puerto Rico's Luis Pales Matos, or the regionalism of Rómulo Gallegos, for example. Mary Louise Pratt has called the self-contradiction of this failed postcolonialism "creole self-fashioning," a kind of unrecognized neocolonial desire to assume the position of the colonizer within one's own nation (172). Primitivism, in this way, silences even as it attempts to give voice to the Other.

The work of scholar Erik Camayd-Freixas, however, points to an important characteristic of some more nuanced forms of primitivism that perhaps warrant our reconsideration. He insists that when primitivism is used to critically examine "*self*-representation" as opposed to mere representation of a non-Western otherness, it can "expose the contradictions of cultural myths and . . . deconstruct the instrumental concepts of identity construction," particularly in response to the positivist and industrial legacies of Latin America's experience of modernity (xviii). As various strategies of primitivism began to expose their own neocolonial paternalism, new and more ironic and self-reflexive strategies emerged, laying bare the gaps between the city and the country, between white and nonwhite populations, and between gendered social positions. What Camayd-Freixas implies is that by the middle of the twentieth century primitivism produced works that investigated and interrogated the very terms of identity—the quintessentiality of such figures as the Indian, the black slave, the guajiro, the gaucho, the mestizo, or the mulatto—upon which modern Latin American nations had sought to found themselves.

For the purposes of this chapter, it is important to note that the desire for the voice of "the primitive" marks early attempts to give voice also to nature in Latin America, since the primitive non-Western figure—either indigenous or black, and not infrequently female—was often conflated with the space of wilderness and the jungle. This means, of course, that the neocolonial trappings of such desires for otherness were not uncommon in relation to nature either. Deep ecologists have insisted on the possibility of an unmediated access to nature's subjectivity and therefore of a biocentric understanding that would redress the violence of anthropocentrism. But as Jorge Marcone reminds us, in the context of Latin America especially, the desire for ecological wisdom cannot be so easily disassociated from a Western desire for the primitive other: "The myth of primitive ecological wisdom is, indeed, a version of the Western myth of the 'noble savage'" (159).[1] The privileging of animism and the essentializing of the native or the black subject can lead to a categorical dismissal of the diasporic subject and of hybridity, and the valorization of wilderness can lead to an unfruitful dismissal of history, technology, and culture.[2]

But if Camayd-Freixas is to be believed, there is a certain power and effectiveness, too, to arguments within cultures seeking postcolonial independence for a thorough reorientation toward those spaces and people who remain on the margins of modernity *as long as these subjects are not rendered ahistorical*. As James Clifford has suggested, Western forms of primitivism fail to challenge the prevailing assumptions and values of colonial culture when the primitive subject is reduced to an ahistorical object, which happens when "the historical relations of power in the work of acquisition are occulted" ("On Collecting," 624). This results in the West's bourgeois desire for fetishized objects, tokens, souvenirs, and other commodities that serve to tame the otherness of the non-Western subject. The hunger for the primitive commodity, whether it be an artifact—or we might argue the fetishized and ahistorical space of wilderness itself—is a false rendering of culture as "enduring, traditional, structural (rather than contingent, syncretic, historical)" (630). Postcolonialism's impulse, as a result, has been to restore historicity to colonialism's wide-ranging fetishes. But Clifford suggests that the Western desire for the primitive can produce new knowledge or new understanding, especially if it is critiqued with an eye toward restoring understanding of the contingency and syncretism of all cultures.

In the example of Alejo Carpentier's *Los pasos perdidos* [*The Lost Steps*], I wish to suggest that a key component to this postcolonial work of historicizing is not just reviving awareness of syncretism and the historical processes by which cultures have emerged in their present and contingent form but also of the ways in which human culture stands in dialectical relationship to ecology. As will become evident, I understand ecology as a space of indeterminacy and instability; it is, of course, the world of ecosystems and their myriad complexes of interdependencies, but as ecologists have argued, it is also a dynamic space of change, imbalance, and even chaos. Because it renders the static boundaries of the human perpetually porous and unstable, an ecologically centered imagination is paradoxically a renunciation of the very idea of a center. Moreover, in this chapter I argue that Carpentier's aesthetic of the New World Baroque strikes a balance that is implied in the term "postcolonial ecology"; it is a balance between ecocriticism's important critique of anthropocentrism and postcolonialism's concern for social justice, what I have elsewhere called a "postcolonial sense of place."[3]

Carpentier revised over several years, beginning in 1949, his theory of *lo real maravilloso* or Latin America's marvelous reality, a belief in the region's fundamentally hybrid character, strange and surprising history, and extraordinary natural environment. He would later connect this marvelous reality to his conception of a New World Baroque, an "inclusive, syncretic, symbiotic" theory of "artistic expression" and of "history and culture" (Zamora, *Magical*, 96). Lois Parkinson Zamora has argued that his baroque aesthetic taps into a predominant characteristic of Latin American experience and sees with what she calls "the inordinate eye." The early manifestations of the New World Baroque in indigenous art and the indigenous and African transculturations evident in colonial architecture and in Latin American music and artistic expression evolved into the neobaroque of twentieth-century Latin American narrative. Zamora characterizes this neobaroque of Latin American fiction as a "self-conscious postcolonial ideology aimed at disrupting entrenched power structures and perceptual categories" (*Inordinate Eye* xvi). Examples of this New World Baroque include Carpentier's contemporary and compatriot José Lezama Lima, Mexico's Carlos Fuentes, and the magical realism of Gabriel García Márquez. Because Carpentier's New World Baroque inherently recognizes nature's unpredictability and strangeness, it does not pretend to control nature but neither does it choose to ignore nature's relevance. Instead of forcing a choice between biocentrism and anthropocentrism, it offers a sense of ecology that is a kind of decentered humanism.

Such notions of ecology have been largely missing from prominent postcolonial critiques of discourses of nature. Thinkers such as Raymond Williams and Mary Louise Pratt have insisted on the historicization of nature in order to expose the human violence hidden by recourse to discourses of the pastoral, "wilderness," and "nature." Pratt, in the recent second edition of *Imperial Eyes*, adds a discussion of Carpentier's notion of *lo real maravilloso*, in which she argues that although he aims toward a more decolonized orientation of cultural authority, his celebration of Latin American marvels collapses into a neocolonial desire for control over cultural meaning on the American side of the Atlantic. Carpentier, she writes, "resolves the neocolonial predicament by re-imagining his relation with Europe as one not of otherness but of authenticity. Through this simultaneously decolonizing and recolonizing gesture, the destination for others becomes a home for a unified white, creole self" (229). Her suspicion toward discourses of "wonder" and the "marvelous," of course, is understandable, given how such praise of nature often disguised colonialism's violent ambition to exploit foreign natural resources.[4] When art praises nature, Williams explains, it does so by means of "a simple extraction of the existence of labourers" (32). To speak of the "innate bounty" and the "natural order" of the country, then, is "an abuse of language" because of the erasure of a laboring human presence (33). Robert Marzec extends the implications of Williams's thesis to insist that British colonialism's aim to rationalize, order, and control across the globe was a symptom of an "ontological dread of undisciplined land" (*Ecological*, 31).

The risk of these arguments, however, is the ease of their own over- generalization. Among other things, historicization also reveals that Williams's English dialectic of city and country or Pratt's imperial eyes are not always operative in the same fashion no matter where we are on the globe, nor with the same ideological and political meaning. If this were the case, historicization and careful interpretation within the context of distinct geographies, cultures, and historical moments would be unnecessary. Stephen Greenblatt warns in *Marvelous Possessions* against an "*a priori* ideological determinism, that is, the notion that particular modes of representation are inherently and necessarily bound to a given culture or class or belief system, and that their effects are unidirectional" (4). He suggests, moreover, that the alternative is not to imagine that representations are always neutral; he stresses the protagonism of cultures and individuals who have "fantastically powerful assimilative mechanisms, mechanisms that work like enzymes to change the ideological composition of foreign bodies" (4).

This flexibility is particularly needed in relation to the question of ecology, lest nature disappear altogether in our critical frames as the ontological fact—separate from the human imagination—that Marzec reminds us it is. In short, nature's nature is that it should never be reduced or equated to its representations.

While it might be difficult to define what nature is, critical readers can at least learn to identify strategies of representation that attempt to respect this ontology. According to Édouard Glissant, successful strategies of this kind render nature dynamic, fluid, and resistant to naming; nature constitutes a character in the story and is never merely background staging for the human drama. It is *terre* not *territoire*. In this regard, Glissant sees something exemplary in Carpentier's novel;[5] we see a modern Western subject of New World history—an aspiring musicologist in New York City who moves to the South American tropics in pursuit of the origin of music—making a mythological journey backward in time from a known geography, *terra nostra*, to a kind of willed, self-consciously denoted unknown, *terra incognita*. It is, in other words, an abdication of the reductive and controlling impulses of naming that in turn liberates the poetic force of language. Glissant suspects that nature's dynamism will more likely exhibit itself in narratives where "landscape in the work stops being merely decorative or supportive and emerges as a full character. Describing the landscape is not enough. *The individual, the community, the land are inextricable in the process of creating history*" (*Caribbean Discourse*, 105 [emphasis added]).

It is this last point that is vital. Glissant describes here a poetic, oneiric function of art that paradoxically emerges from an attempt to mimetically describe and represent a New World reality. This "aesthetics of disruption and intrusion" imagines the shape of overlapping histories of violence *and* the force of ecology itself but in so doing becomes not a copy of the world but a poetics, a world-(re)making. This means that representation attributes meaning to human experience and to the environment without making a summative or totalized claim on that meaning (*Poetics* 151); human experience and ecology are instead imagined in meaningful yet tentative relation. To insist that nature is "always a form of social knowledge," though true, is also, as Nancy Stepan points out, "almost a cliché" because critics have wanted to reduce nature merely to its social meaning. To fail to see, or to refuse belief in, anything at work in culture beyond social meaning means we have condemned ourselves to a solipsistic and anthropocentric theory of culture. It would seem we are condemned only and always to see ourselves in the mirror of nature we create. What is needed is an added consideration of the fact that nature is not *only* a form of social knowledge but also always performing a challenge to social knowledge.[6]

THE MARVELOUS REALITY OF LATIN AMERICAN LITERATURE

Ironically, the fact that nature appeared Edenic to scientists, authors, and other members of the literate elite in nineteenth-century Latin America was itself already a symptom of human-caused environmental cataclysms in the age of Conquest. These events included widespread, unprecedented and exceptional disease, enforced labor and enslavement, violent displacement of peoples and cultures, and the transplantation of Africans, Europeans, European flora and fauna, and Asian plants and peoples. As Shawn Miller points out, the population of the Americas wouldn't reach pre-1492 levels until the twentieth century; Latin America was more forested in 1800 than it was in 1492, and it saw greater biodiversity than its precolonial past until its rapid demise in the age of modernization in the late nineteenth and early twentieth centuries. Environmental history like Miller's not only insists on the historicity of nature; it also makes the case for the ecological foundations of human history and, for my purposes here, for the ecological dimensions of *literary* history. Latin American modernism's varied attempts to ground Latin American authenticity in regional soils resulted in ironic portrayals of the limits of representation; nature's ontology—its dynamic ecology—proved consistently resistant to its capture in language or image.

The modernism of Alejo Carpentier (1904–80) is characterized by a sustained argument against European modernism and its discontents.[7] Born in Cuba to a French father and a mother of Russian descent, Carpentier was a polyglot, a world traveler, and a man of extraordinary erudition regarding Western art, literature, and music history. But he was also devoted to the cause of a cultural and political liberation of Latin America and his native Cuba. As evident in his theory of *lo real maravilloso* [the marvelous reality of Latin America] and the New World Baroque, his profound awareness of the particular racial, political, geographical, and cultural history of his region of the world convinced him that the postcoloniality of Latin American culture lay in its willingness to give form and shape to its lived experience.

It was accepted wisdom, at least since the nineteenth century, that Latin America's liberation turned on this willingness to engage in the praxis of mimesis. The colonial condition of Latin American culture, as many saw it, was most evident in a patent disregard for the local particulars of the Americas and a preference for the patterns and precedents set by European and U.S. trends. By the late nineteenth century, artists had begun to experiment with a kind of hermeneutics of recovery, scanning local landscapes, histories, and peoples for signs of difference from this colonial legacy. This would culminate in the movements of regionalism, indigenism, and negritude of the early twentieth century and the staunch insistence that Latin America, as a transnational entity, was inherently mestizo. This new Latin Americanism sought to be more authentic and overtly postcolonial than the earlier attempts of cultural liberation in the nineteenth century even though it resulted at times in a well-documented paternalism and continued marginalization of more radical voices of regional and racial difference. Carpentier's theory of *lo real maravilloso*, first articulated in his 1949 prologue to his novel about the Haitian Revolution, *El reino de este mundo* [*The Kingdom of This World*], took this project to capture and valorize the local to a more nuanced and much-needed level of poetic self-ironizing.

The marvelous, for Carpentier, is the experience of surprise and wonder in an encounter with utter strangeness; it is "the awareness of being Other, of being new, of being symbiotic, of being a *criollo*; and the *criollo* spirit is itself a baroque spirit" ("Baroque," 100). This, of course, was akin to the pursuit of much of European modernism and surrealism in particular, but Carpentier insists, "if Surrealism pursued the marvelous, one would have to say that it very rarely looked for it in reality" (103). For Carpentier and his compatriot Wifredo Lam, surrealism was not wrong to want to counterpose a "soul-less, urban modernity" with a "natural frenzy," a "living, animated jungle" (Wilson, 78); the problem was that this jungle for the European was more imagined than experienced and therefore a mere rhetorical trick, a first-world fantasy about the third world. The Latin American's closer proximity to the jungle, of course, doesn't guarantee an escape from fantasies of primitivism. To experience wonder is to experience eccentricity, to be outside of the center of phenomena one experiences.

The perhaps unintended consequence of Carpentier's theory is that even though it produces the same eccentricity that surrealism couldn't overcome, because it more overtly commits itself to the objective of mimesis—of direct confrontation and experience with the tropics—human consciousness is understood as eccentric in relation to an unnamed but dynamically present biological center. The saving grace of this relationship is how ecology is a world without a center, as I already indicated, and therefore disrupts and renders perpetually contingent the binary of center and periphery. For Carpentier, surrealism's effect of strangeness was calculated and prefabricated (Salvador Dalí's melting clocks, for example); it did not start with the intention to be mimetic since European modernism did not have the confidence that reality itself would provide the experience of strangeness.[8] Carpentier's theory, on the other hand, was inherently mundane; it found its greatest potency and, as I will argue, its richest ironies, in what in *The Lost Steps* Carpentier refers to as "Adam's task of giving things their names." This is direct experience with the "raw state" of the "commonplace" and in the "untamed" and "unruly complexities of [New World] nature and its vegetation, the many colors that surround us, the telluric pulse of the phenomena that we still feel" ("Baroque," 104, 105). As opposed to the Old World Baroque that was born out of the Counter-Reformation and was so closely allied with Catholic aesthetics, José Lezama Lima similarly saw the New World baroque as more centered in, and hence decentered by, nature: the Old World baroque was fashioned to facilitate "a rationalistic elaboration of the city" whereas the American baroque "raised . . . the wealth of nature over and above monetary wealth . . . in such a way, that even within Hispanic poverty, lies the wealth of American matter [material]" (50).[9] The resistant force of the New World baroque "is nourished, in its very purity, by the gusts of the true American forest" (56).[10]

This mimeticism of the New World Baroque did not produce naïve neo-Romantic nature writing, however. Although centered on a description on the physical world, what emerges is not a copy but a new world made by "a new vocabulary" and "a new optic" required to see the environment one inhabits (Carpentier, "Baroque," 105). In this sense, a baroque response to the world is both faithful and treacherous; it centers and decenters the self. For Carpentier, it helps that tropical nature itself appears to be characterized by the baroque "horror of the vacuum, the naked surface, the harmony of lineary geometry." The New World baroque is eccentric in that it "moves outward and away from the center, [it] somehow breaks through its own borders," and it is only because so too does the biological world (93). As he explains, "If our duty is to depict the world, we must uncover and interpret it ourselves. Our reality will appear new to our own eyes. Description is inescapable, and the description of a baroque world is necessarily baroque, that is, in this case the *what* and the *how* coincide in a baroque reality" (106). Baroque representation leaves us with two worlds, linked but apart—the world and a represented world and a split awareness that poiesis and mimesis are intertwined and inseparable but never identical.[11] While this is arguably true of all representation, baroque forms seem to offer a particularly self-reflective method of assessing one's eccentricity, or outsideness, vis-à-vis an extravagant ecological reality within which one is nevertheless embedded.

In her description of the differences in the role of representation in indigenous and European art, Lois Parkinson Zamora notes that European tradition has favored the control of the observing "I/eye," a subject that remains separate from and not participatory in the world that is represented, whereas indigenous forms of representation seek to be "*image-as-presence*," inseparable from the seeing subject (*Inordinate*, 15). In the former, mimesis predominates, in the latter poiesis. She writes, "The conventions of Western perspective . . . remind viewers of the image's *likeness to* nature and, hence, our *separation from* nature. Western perspective frames what is seen from outside the framed scene, thus encoding the seer's detachment from the visible world" (15). Ecocriticism has sought to identify ways of seeing that do not result in this separation but that also do not erase or obscure the human agency in giving representative form to nature. It would seem that Zamora's definition of the "inordinate eye" works as one such method.

As Amaryll Chanady notes, in its aggressive inclusiveness of different orders of seeing, Carpentier's notion of America's marvelous reality "does not occupy a distinct area of literary production separate from that of mimetic writing, as does the marvelous domain of fairy tales [or the fabricated methods of surrealism, for Carpentier]. . . . On the contrary, the mode challenges realistic representation in order to introduce *poiesis* into *mimesis*" (130). What accounts for this new method of representation is not "a naïve essentialist argument" that sees Latin American exceptionalism—its history of racial mixture, its political violence, its uneven development, or even its extraordinary geography—as the rule that determines this cultural outcome; after all, an environmentally determined culture can hardly be conceived to be liberatory. This new method is, rather, a combination of attentive description of the particulars of one's environment and of self-willed creation of a new world. This combination makes of a work of representation something both *of* nature and *like* nature. Ecologically centered art is ambiguously both separate from and part of the world and is the vehicle by which we explore and understand our belonging in the more-than-human cosmos. While one might insist on the postcolonial value of *lo real maravilloso*, this ambiguity makes it also ecologically valuable.

THE NATURE OF CARPENTIER'S BAROQUE WORLD

In 1947 and 1948, Carpentier made two voyages of several weeks in duration to the Amazonian interior of the Orinoco watershed, the same territory that had inspired Sir Alfred Conan Doyle and Jules Verne, the lands of El Dorado. These voyages would later find fictional form in *The Lost Steps*. What he came to appreciate was that culture has a tendency to grow impatient with and distant from the dynamism of the natural world, at its own peril. In a column he wrote for *El Nacional* in Venezuela months before the publication of *The Lost Steps* and after his voyages, he insists on a commitment to a dialectic contact and comparison between the space of the city and the space of nature:

> The tentacular cities—as the poet Verhaeren calls them—New York, Philadelphia . . . produce a kind of man, son of modern times, who inspires in me an infinite pity. He is the one who passes months of the year without having any contact with nature. . . . For me, such an existence—which is the existence of millions and millions in this world—is an intimation [prefiguración] of hell. Moreover, I cannot bring myself to believe that it is worth living in such a manner. Without frequent contact with nature, man forgets who he is, he is sterilized, loses his vital rhythms, he becomes distrustful of his own biology [se hace desconfiado ante la propia carne]. In his labyrinths of reinforced concrete, in his pathways of asphalt, he comes to forget, as well, the very sky that exists overhead—a round and true sky, not framed by the stony edges of

> buildings [la estereotomía de los edificios]. [This man] knows a little bit about everything . . . but he has forgotten the names of the stars." ("Presencia" August 23, 1952)[12]

Carpentier was intent on revising Romanticism for a modern Latin America whose natural wonders had made little difference in the formation of Latin American culture. As he suggests in another column, however, the difference in Latin America is the nature of the tropics, nature on a scale that defies description, shatters illusions of pastoral balance, and terrifies the onlooker into a kind of muted submission ("El turista"). He notes, "America still lives beneath the telluric sign of the great storms and great floods. There will always be some meteorological role, from Miami, Havana, the Grand Cayman islands, to remind us that our nature has not yet become so 'friendly,' so tranquil like Goethe would have wanted the whole world to be—in the image of his romantic Germany" ("Presencia" October 2, 1952).[13]

His expedition to the Amazonian interior of the Orinoco delta in 1947 fanned the flames of this desire to lay claim to a still relatively untamed and unknown natural world, but it also brought him into contact with the people and cultures of the region and the jungle's potent and defiant telluric ontology. One can hardly miss the ways in which *The Lost Steps* is a fable of a twentieth-century neocolonial and masculine conquest and mapping of *terrae incognitae*. His frequent use of the clichéd "virgin" nature both in his essays and in the novel attest to this masculinist temptation, as we will see. However, he is generally more drawn to the idea of nature as Genesis rather than Eden. That is, nature is not static or passive but is instead a kind of ongoing creation—what he calls a "perennial 'revelation of forms'" (*Visión*, 33)—demonstrating an ecological dynamism that defies linguistic control. As we see, this generative force has the effect of destabilizing the tropic and neocolonial methods of the white, metropolitan man in *The Lost Steps*. As Timothy Morton notes, nature "keeps giving writers the slip" (2); that the mimetic attempt results in a poetics suggests, ultimately, that a more ecological understanding of human being requires a critical apparatus that is interested in critiquing more than just the socially-constructed self. Moreover, this human ecology becomes a cross-cultural poetics that is a mode of imagining the whole complex overlay of divergent mythologies, desires, and experiences with nature that inform Latin American experience. Inasmuch as *lo real maravilloso* relies on a position of outsidedness, it can play into the fantasies of the Western traveler whose externality relies on the privilege of travel, of mobility, and access to comparative cultural and geographical contexts. But its more profound implication is that ethical experience between diverse human subjects and the natural world should remain *intersubjective*, multiplied and decentered by an awareness of the contingencies of the singular seeing I/eye.

THE LOST STEPS TO AN UNNAMEABLE NATURE

Carpentier's unnamed male protagonist in *The Lost Steps* is the quintessence of the unhappy modern. A composer and academic, he is unhappy in marriage as well as in his liaison with a pseudo-intellectual mistress with whom he leaves the fatigue and "automatism" of a northern American city, presumably New York, and arrives among the tribes of the Amazonian interior of the upper Orinoco in order to prove that the foundations of music lie in the mimetic impulse to copy the sounds of nature (5). New York and Caracas, where he stays temporarily, are characterized by an architecture of the urban baroque, similar to Lezama Lima's description, where a rationalization "falsif[ies] the reality of proportions, establishing a scale of their own, like constructions designed for some unfamiliar use" despite the fact that "for hundreds of years a struggle had been going on with roots that pushed up the sidewalks and cracked the walls" (38). As he gets farther away from urban life, he is struck by the fact that the world's metropolitan centers are "museum cities," founded on commemorating what resists nature's ravaging erosions (65). This resembles, of course, the very opposition between city and country that Raymond Williams challenges, but in a Latin American context "country" is not imagined to be the pastoral space of human harmony with the landscape but the barbarism the nineteenth-century writer and Argentine politician Domingo Faustino Sarmiento once associated with the untamed spaces outside the law. Carpentier wants to challenge Sarmiento's dichotomy between civilization and barbarism by exposing not only the marginalized nonurban subjects but the wild ecology that the rationality of the city has not learned to tolerate.

Initially, however, it seems his narrator has found in the jungle his ideal object of nonurban otherness. Once he arrives at the Amazonian interior, he falls under Rosario's spell, a simple, uneducated woman in whom "several races had met [varias razas se encontraban mezcladas] . . . Indian in the hair and cheekbones, Mediterranean in brow and nose, Negro in the heavy shoulders and the breadth of the hips" (81/147).[14] In over-the-top primitivist and sexist rhetoric, he describes her as a veritable "living sum of races [viviente suma de razas]," the "great races of the world," which history had separated for centuries and which "had ignored the fact that they inhabited the same planet" (82/147). Unlike Mouche, his surrealist mistress, or Ruth, his actress wife, she seems to be the very emblem of a pastoral possibility because she always "established links with her surroundings [establecer con el ambiente ciertas relaciones]" (106/170); she is a "woman of the earth" (180). To the narrator, Rosario moves according to natural rhythms, is an avatar of ancient peoples and lifeways, and with her, sexual intimacy and work in a tropical pastoral village become a kind of sacrament (173). The protagonist sees her as the ultimate antidote to modern mobility, urbanity, and angst, the very trope of the receptive native woman who welcomes the Western outsider.

Significantly, as the protagonist advances into the jungle and into his relationship with Rosario, he begins to find this attributed symbolic meaning slipping from his control. This is concomitant with his growing awareness that nature's generative powers defy his capacity to give adequate representation to its various forms. The baroque qualities of the jungle are evident in its "disconcerting and new" forms, its "blind geometry" (119, 138). Unlike an easy German Romantic pastoral or the passive and static notion of an Eden discussed earlier, he insists the jungle is more akin to the pre-Edenic moment of Genesis, the "diabolical vegetation that surrounded the Garden of Eden before the Fall." He finds himself observing a

> kind of crater in whose depths horrendous plants proliferated. They were like fleshy grasses whose morbid shoots were round like tentacles or arms. The huge leaves, open like hands, resembled submarine flora in their texture of coral and seaweed, with bulbous flowers like feather lanterns, birds suspended from a vein, ears of corn of larvae, bloodshot pistils bursting from their sides [por un proceso de erupción y desgarre] without the grace of a stem. And all this, there below, intertwined, tangled, in a grappling, coupling, monstrous and orgiastic, incests that represent the supreme confusion of forms. (205/265)

Note that the strange and almost terrifying proliferation of forms leads to a similarly "blind geometry" of proliferating similes and metaphors. Baroque nature leads to baroque prose, but this is not mere mimeticism at work, precisely because of the ways in which nature's monstrous biodiversity is its incestuousness; ecology does not promise facile, predictable, or measurable reproduction or classification to appease male desire, but instead confuses forms and eludes his desire, leaving him conscious of his own figural language. As he contemplates the hundreds of thousands of unnamed species, the narrator laments that "this fearful density of leaves [ese tremendo espesor de hojas] . . . would one day disappear from the planet without having been given a name, without having been re-created by the Word [por la palabra]" (206/266). Adam's task of naming is really re-creation, more like Noah after the deluge; unnameable nature—which he here compares to the same "blank *terra incognita* of the old cartographers" in the colonial period—provides endless "stimuli to thought, motives for meditation, forms of art, poetry, myth, more helpful to the understanding of man than hundreds of books written by men who pride themselves on knowing Man" (208–9). The narrator's unmistakable male desire turns away from the ambition of naming as possession toward that of the poiesis of artistic expression.

Elsewhere the narrator insists that this confusion leads to "a kind of disorientation, and a dizziness of the eyes [mareo de los ojos]. It was no longer possible to say which was tree and which reflection of tree. Was the light coming from above or below? Was the sky or the earth water?" (161/223).[15] He remarks, "What amazed me most was the inexhaustible mimetism of virgin nature [el inacabable mimetismo de la naturaleza virgen]. Everything here seemed something else, thus creating a world of appearances that concealed reality, casting doubts on many truths" (165/227). One of the truths that the ecology of baroque nature confuses is the reliable and identifiable distinction between human and more-than-human meaning. At several junctures the narrator is confused about whether he is seeing evidence of human ruins or simply natural forms that mimic and mock memorials to a human past, "as though some strange civilization of people different from those we know had flourished there" (138). So "virgin" nature starts to lose its gendered and sexualized meaning and take on the attributes of a space of such regenerative force that the tropes aimed at controlling nature's meaning lose their structure. If nature is indeed hiding a human history (which, of course, it was), its fecundity marginalizes, decenters humanity; as a result, language takes on the character of hopeful and rhetorical guesswork. Moreover, Carpentier implies that a decentered humanity in a biological cosmos in which boundaries are uncertain presents an opportunity for a postcolonial inclusion of differences expelled by colonial desire. He asks "whether perhaps the role of these lands in the history of man might not be to make possible for the first time certain symbioses of cultures" (119–20).

Representation as probing and investigative guesswork means that it becomes more rhetorical, self-reflexive, and hence less about recovering the "primitive" and the "wild" but more about understanding and respecting the contours and limitations of human cultures in an intersubjective and more-than-human context. Carpentier's point is that nature's value is precisely that it delineates these limitations, but only *after*, paradoxically, the artist first aspires to escape the trappings of culture and recover nature's rawness.

Initially the protagonist believes that music was born of imitation of natural sound, but while watching a tribe of Indians mourning over the body of a fallen hunter, he alters his theory. Art, he concludes, is

> the earliest attempt [intento primordial] to combat the forces of annihilation which frustrate man's designs. . . . Before the stubbornness of Death, which refused to release its prey, the Word suddenly grew faint and disheartened. In the mouth of the shaman, the spell-working orifice, the *Threne*—for that was what this was—gasped and died away convulsively, blinding me with the realization [dejándome deslumbrado con la revelación] that I had just witnessed the Birth of Music. (184–85/245)

All forms of artistic representation come to represent a response to or an awareness of the reality of death, which he shows in the novel is a confrontation with the biological facts that underlie our existence and consciousness.[16] To merely love picturesque nature, to praise its beauty and believe in a facile harmony between humankind and nature, is a shallow Romanticism that denies the passage and ravages of time. Carpentier's tropical world is not merely surprising because it is beautiful; it is marvelous because it is "implacable, terrible, in spite of its beauty" (195). Carpentier seems to presciently anticipate conceptions of chaos in ecology since the 1960s; the horror that nature's violence inspires makes it hard to argue for a harmonious notion of biocentrism where all life-forms are on an equal plane; humanity—or at least the narrator's white male and erudite version of humanity—uses artistic representation to see with Zamora's "inordinate eye." This is a way of temporarily stepping aside so as to see himself within this newfound, broader context. The baroque offers a contingent biocentrism, just as his is now a more contingent self-reflective male desire. Although nature's violence is not as fearsome to those who live with it, the pastoral dream of harmony between nature and culture is no longer possible since

> the plagues, the possible sufferings, the natural dangers [must be] accepted as a matter of course [de antemano]; they formed part of an Order that had its severity [sus rigores]. Creation is no laughing matter, and [those whose life is spent with it] all knew and accepted the role each of them had been assigned in the great tragedy of living [de lo creado]. But it was a tragedy with a unity of time, place, and action; in it, death itself operated under the direction of known masters, attired in poisons, scale, fire, miasmas, to the accompaniment of the thunder and lightning. (195/256)

By implication, then, anything that denies human biology or human locality in the physical world will not provide a sufficient confrontation with human contingency, temporality, and mortality and therefore cannot sufficiently nurture an awareness of ethics. Representation that accepts the biological reality of death, of unpredictable change, of surprising beauty and horror, is art attuned to the minute changes and formal dynamism of ecology, an ever-dying, regenerative, and hence baroque, world. This is the reason that this ecological awareness, although ostensibly focusing the eye and ear to the physical world and therefore mimetic in intention, is self-reflexive and poetic in result.

The narrator composes his own masterpiece, his own Threnody and expression of mourning over death, as a tribute to this new awareness. He feels that this work represents the very renewal of civilization the automatism of his former life needed, but his failure pertains to the very material contingencies of a physical, biological world that inspired him. Even the life of the music depends on the dead body of a tree: paper. He needs more paper than he can find in the jungle to make it into a transferable and communicable thing. When an opportunity presents itself to return to New York, he takes the trip, intending to return with paper to complete his notes, which he leaves with Rosario. Neither she nor his manuscript is ever seen again.

His artistic failure is the culmination of a growing awareness of Rosario's eluctability. She becomes more distant and, showing more self-possession than he had thought she had, ultimately refuses to marry him. This causes him to consider that his sexual desires are pornographic, which he defines as "the degradation and distortion of all that might contribute . . . to a man's finding compensation for his failures in the affirmation of his virility, achieving his fullest realization in the flesh he divides" (99). After witnessing the arrival to the village of a young girl raped by a leper, he is given the chance to shoot the leper in punishment. He declines and admits his own pornographic desire: "The disgust and indignation I felt at the outrage was unspeakable; it was as though I, a man, all men, were equally guilty of this revolting attempt because of the mere fact that possession, even willing [consentida], puts the male in the attitude of aggression" (230/288).

This admission of guilt comes after pages of elaborate descriptions of the sexual energy he discovers in Rosario's companionship and after his voyage into the jungle has already been cast in unmistakably sexual terms. Early in the novel when he first arrives in the jungle, the travelers who accompany him look for a passage—unmistakably cast as a vagina—through a forest of mangroves, "without sign of an opening, without a cleavage, without a crevice" until they find a tree marked with three vertical V's next to which lies the narrow passage into the womblike interior jungle (159). At the novel's conclusion, when he comes back to the jungle to find Rosario, he cannot locate the entrance because the sign has been buried by the river's higher waters, much to his dismay at being obstructed by "such an absurd contingency [tan absurdo contratiempo]" (270/323). To add insult to injury, after Rosario had told him she wouldn't marry him because she wishes to remain free, he learns that she has married in the village while he has been gone. The protagonist's journey ends in resolute failure.

CONCLUSION

My reading is not meant to suggest that Carpentier's theory of Latin American culture is inoculated in some way against the pitfalls of neocolonialism. Carpentier's binary of the city and the jungle exhibits many of the trappings of male colonial desire, and his insistence on the return to the feminized primitive and the wild in order to escape the artificial city is at times environmentally naïve. An ecocritical reading of this structure therefore risks reinventing the very opposition between nature and culture that New World history has rendered ambiguous. But we have to take that ambiguity seriously, and that means that we cannot know for sure what is natural and what is cultural. If the nature/culture binary becomes an *important but rhetorical differentiation*, then ecocriticism's interest in a return to nature can be understood as an advocacy of a kind of ritualistic performance, a self-conscious re-creation of the world, that keeps the human subject and human representations answerable to a world that cannot be possessed.

If ecocriticism asks us to ontologize in the interest of determining the proper human relationship to nature, postcolonialism urges us to historicize. Perhaps they both point to a kind of contingent ontology, an awareness that, as Carpentier argues, no culture can escape from the pitfalls of colonialism's commodification and binarization of the world without at least risking an appeal to nature. Yet we cannot approach the jungle as anything but human subjects—male, female, white, black, European, native, members of a social class, and so on—so there is no escaping the ways in which these factors shape and inform our desire for nature's otherness. Culture needs nature in order to remain creative and alive, but culture needs also to remain apart and deferential, lest we render nature objectified, falsely believed to be known and possessed, by our human discourse. An ecological ethos renounces all claims to authenticity and stasis founded on historical continuity, tradition, and habit. Carpentier's poetics is not the possessive impulse of colonial cultures and museum cities that fetishize and commodify nature and "primitives" outside of time and change; instead it portrays a culture founded on the paradoxical acceptance of the fact that it will be perpetually transformed by nature's indifferent erosions. Such indifference forces Carpentier's protagonist to renounce Rosario and the jungle as the static answers to Latin America's postcolonial quest he thought they were. His postcolonialism is oriented to the ecological margins precisely to the degree that he accepts the paradox of this renunciation. His own appeal to an ecological imagination becomes "an aesthetics of disruption," to borrow from Glissant. The only possession taken from the jungle is not the protagonist's *magnum opus* of the Threnody; it is instead Carpentier's novel in our hands, what in the novel he suggests is really an urn, a work at least thrice removed from the natural order that inspired it—once by the narrator's parallel world he created in the music, twice by virtue of the narrative acting as the music's substitute, and thrice by virtue of its function as a rhetorical representation of a fictional narrator. Wendy Faris notes that Carpentier's novel, like William Faulkner's "The Bear," represents an attempt "at the appropriation of land by text that [is] ultimately unsatisfactory, not only because of flawed motivations but because of the impossibility of the task" (252). The failure, she explains, "is only mediated by the [text] we are reading. Words bridge the gap between the two realms, giving access to the truths of the heart and the rhythms of nature learned in the primordial realm so that they are remembered in the city." Because of the self-ironizing that results from the confrontation of the nature/culture divide, she insists that Carpentier's protagonist "comes to [an] explicit recognition of his delusions" (253). In this sense the novel, and perhaps any ecologically oriented postcolonial work, is a *memento mori*, an expression of mourning, or recompense, for the mortal facts of human biology.

Carpentier's novel feels timely in both senses; it is relevant for contemporary concerns with ecology even as it also feels dated. Carpentier was not able to fully transcend the reactionary naturalism of earlier primitivism in Latin America that invoked the tropics, women, Indians, and blacks as reified opposites to European metropolitanism, but perhaps we would do well to exercise our readerly agency and imagine, as Amaryll Chanady does, that *lo real maravilloso* is a territorialization of the marvelously real; that is, instead of offering essential racial or gender difference or essential nature as sites of postcolonial resistance, it is a *rhetorical* performance or localization of a postcolonial ethos that values difference *deferentially*. A sense of ecology becomes both mimetic *and* poetic when art temporarily territorializes nature—as a sign of value—but then renounces its ability to subsume and capture it—as a sign of respect. In this perpetual dialogue between the physical word and human consciousness, the pathologies of believing in radical human naturalism, on the one hand, and of believing in radical human separatism, on the other, are thus both kept at bay. In postcolonial terms, this means that Latin America's diversity, size, and the simultaneity of its various cultures and geographies can generate cultural difference and autonomy while it also delimits that very culture ecologically. If Latin America's reality cannot generate cultural difference, it can hardly be trusted to offer an adequate answer to the legacies of colonialism. But neither can we consider it adequate if it does not result in a sense of ecology, since colonialism degrades cultures and ecosystems alike. Only a postcolonial ecology, then, holds the key to New World originality.

I would like to thank: Luisa Campuzano and her colleagues in Havana who attended my seminar on ecocriticism and provided stimulating feedback in July 2008; Jorge Marcone, my collaborator on the seminar; Araceli García-Carranza Bassetti at the Biblioteca Nacional in Havana; Lois Parkinson Zamora and Wendy Faris, who read drafts and offered careful criticism; Ursula Heise, a marvelous critic, and the Penn State Americanists who supported my visit to campus; Luis Valente and Rex Nielson who invited a presentation on the topic at Brown University; and Elizabeth DeLoughrey, for her tough and important criticisms.

NOTES

1. On the ways in which this desire is also informed by gender, see especially the works of Carolyn Merchant and Annette Kolodny.

2. In readings of such writers as Horacio Quiroga, Benito Lynch, and Eustasio Rivera, Jennifer French marks the persistence of neocolonial desire for the tropics among Latin American regionalists that parallels the structures of British colonialism in nineteenth- and early twentieth-century Latin America.

3. See my essay "A Postcolonial Sense of Place in the Work of Derek Walcott." This idea receives full treatment in my book, *New World Poetics*, and represents a kind of ecological poetics of diaspora, a way of imagining the importance of place and of nature but that also attends to a mitigation of the social hierarchies that a sense of place often generates. This kind of dual critical attention is exemplified by Sarah Casteel in her book *Second Arrivals* and in Elizabeth DeLoughrey's *Routes and Roots*. Casteel warns that diaspora theory "tends . . . to polarize mobility and sedentarism, often celebrating the former while neglecting, or even disparaging, the latter" (2).

4. This is the particularly important contribution of French's aforementioned ecocritical study of Latin American literature, in which she assiduously identifies the mystifications of landscape that have served to erase the hand of British and U.S. neocolonialism in the region.

5. See in particular Glissant's *Caribbean Discourse*, 81–82.

6. See my chapter, "New World Poetics," in *New World Poetics*.

7. For an examination of Carpentier's intricate response to Andre Breton and the surrealists, particularly the reasons for his adaptation of Breton's title, *Les Pas perdus*, see Jason Wilson. Wilson suggests that Carpentier was critical of surrealism's denial of history and desire to "start the whole enterprise from a violent *tabula rasa*" (71).

8. A famous anecdote about the surrealism of Andre Breton tells of his debate with Roger Caillois about a Mexican jumping bean. Caillois insisted that one should cut open the bean and solve the mystery of its movement while Breton preferred to remain in ignorance of the science in order to let his poetic imagination run free. Breton has created a false dichotomy, assuming that the biological facts of existence could not themselves warrant poetry, wonder, and estrangement.

9. Translation mine. All translations not indicated in the bibliography are my translations.

10. In *New World Poetics*, I have elaborated on the ways in which nature renders this Christian and gendered notion of the poet as Adam contingent and the extent to which it manages to avoid the excesses of the colonialist desire for untamed nature.

11. Timothy Morton notes that ecology inherently challenges the very binaries of self and environment, human and natural, natural and supernatural, that are operative in much environmental thought. What is important to recognize, for Morton, is that we can never definitively name nature, or as he puts it, "we cannot point to it" (18). In our desire to find that place where we are no longer apart from it, we "go on generating binary pairs, and we would always *be coming down on one side or the other, missing the exact center*" (19 [emphasis mine]). By definition, then, biocentrism produces eccentricities indefinitely.

12. These columns are archived at the Biblioteca Nacional in Havana.

13. Carpentier is not above neocolonial desire to appropriate the marvelous—without irony—in the interest of a pure Latin American originality, of course, and this is his great temptation. One column reports on a recent publication of the explorations of Alain Gheerbrant, who discovered several large petroglyphs in the interior that left Gheerbrant speechless. Carpentier insists that Gheerbrant stood "before a new fact, absolutely original, in the history of primitive art" ("Gran Libro"). Another column expresses intense excitement and vindication since Angel Falls—the longest waterfall in the world in the Amazonian interior of Venezuela—had finally appeared in the *National Geographic* ("Misterios"). The spectacle of the falls promises mysteries yet to be named and discovered. Carpentier remarks, "It is a Lost World, more moving than all of the imagined worlds of Conan Doyle" ("Misterios"). Jules Vernes's 1898 novel, *The Mighty Orinoco*, is the subject of two other columns, and in both cases his purpose is to strike a contrast between the inauthenticity of European representations and the authentic reality that is Latin America's own inheritance. Margarita Mateo Palmer notes that in *Los pasos perdidos*, Carpentier demonstrates that such myths are not the sole property of the European imagination but have different valences, origins, and meanings in indigenous contexts in Latin America, making something like El Dorado a "mobile, migratory myth" (153).

14. Where the original Spanish is indicated for added clarification, I have listed a second page number for the Spanish edition.

15. In Carpentier's papers at the Biblioteca Nacional in Havana, one finds a photo album of pictures that Carpentier took during his 1947 voyage to the Upper Orinoco and the Gran Sabana. Among the photos are several images of the river's still shoreline reflecting identical forms above and below, illustrating precisely his fascination with this sense of disorientation.

16. Robert Harrison's *Forests* suggests that the very forms of representation we use in language to structure meaning stand in a delicate and tenuous balance with the forests, the spaces of perpetual and indifferent ecological regeneration. Because the forest is the space against which language—and civilization itself—structures itself, it is the space of death and silence. "Nature knows how to die," he writes, "but human beings know mostly how to kill as a way of failing to become our ecology" (249). To become our ecology means to reorient civilization toward the forest, to use language to "speak our death to the world" or to approach an acceptance of the biological facts of our existence, including an embrace of human mortality.

WORKS CITED

Camayd-Freixas, Erik. "Introduction: The Returning Gaze." In *Primitivism and Identity in Latin America: Essays on Art, Literature, and Culture*, edited by Erik Camayd-Freixas and José Eduardo González, vii–xix. University of Arizona Press, 2000.

Carpentier, Alejo. "The Baroque and the Marvelous Real." In *Magical Realism: Theory, History, Community*, edited by Lois Parkinson Zamora and Wendy B. Faris, 89–108. Durham: Duke University Press, 1995.

———. "El Gran Libro de la Selva." *El Nacional*. May 14, 1952. [Caracas].

———. *The Lost Steps*. Translated by Harriet de Onís. New York: Noonday Press, 1989.

———. "Misterios de la Naturaleza Venezolana." *El Nacional*. July 21, 1952. [Caracas].

———. "On the Marvelous Real in America." In *Magical Realism: Theory, History, Community*, edited by Lois Parkinson Zamora and Wendy B. Faris, 75–88. Durham: Duke University Press, 1995.

———. *Los pasos perdidos*. Madrid: Catedra Letras Hispánicas, 1985.

———. "Presencia de la naturaleza." *El Nacional*. August 23, 1952. [Caracas].

———. "Presencia de la naturaleza." *El Nacional*. October 2, 1952. [Caracas].

———. *El reino de este mundo*. New York: Rayo, 2009.

———. "El turista y el viajero." *El Nacional*. October 21, 1952. [Caracas].

———. *Visión de América: fragmentos de una crónica de viajes*. Buenos Aires: Losada, 1999.

Chanady, Amaryll. "The Territorialization of the Imaginary in Latin America: Self-Affirmation and Resistance to Metropolitan Paradigms." In *Magical Realism: Theory, History, Community*, edited by Lois Parkinson Zamora and Wendy B. Faris, 125–44. Duke University Press, 1995.

Clifford, James. "On Collecting Art and Culture." In *Art and Its Significance: An Anthology of Aesthetic Theory*, edited by Stephen David Ross, 621–42. State University of New York Press, 1994.

Faris, Wendy. "Marking Space, Charting Time: Text and Territory in Faulkner's 'The Bear' and Carpentier's *Los Pasos Perdidos*." In *Do the Americas Have a Common Literature?* edited by Gustavo Pérez-Firmat, 243–65. Duke University Press, 1990.

Glissant, Édouard. *Caribbean Discourse: Selected Essays*. Translated by J. Michael Dash. University Press of Virginia, 1989.

———. *Poetics of Relation*. Translated by Betsy Wing. University of Michigan Press, 1997.

Greenblatt, Stephen. *Marvelous Possessions: The Wonder of the New World*. University of Chicago Press, 1991.

Marcone, Jorge. "Jungle Fever: Primitivism in Environmentalism: Rómulo Gallego's Canaima and the Romance of the Jungle." In *Primitivism and Identity in Latin America: Essays on Art, Literature, and Culture*, edited by Erik Camayd-Freixas and José Eduardo González, 157–72. University of Arizona Press, 2000.

Marzec, Robert. *An Ecological and Postcolonial Study of Literature: From Daniel Defoe to Salman Rushdie*. Palgrave, 2007.

Miller, Shawn. *An Environmental History of Latin America*. Cambridge University Press, 2007.

Morton, Timothy. *Ecology without Nature: Rethinking Environmental Aesthetics*. Harvard University Press, 2007.

Pratt, Mary Louise. *Imperial Eyes: Travel Writing and Transculturation*. 2nd ed. Routledge, 1992; 2008.

Stepan, Nancy. *Picturing Tropical Nature*. Cornell University Press, 2001.
Williams, Raymond. *The Country and the City*. Oxford University Press, 1975.
Wilson, Jason. "Alejo Carpentier's Re-invention of América Latina as Real and Marvellous." In *A Companion to Magical Realism*, edited by Stephen M. Hart and Wen-Chin Ouyang, 67–78. Tamesis, 2005.
Zamora, Lois Parkinson. *The Inordinate Eye: New World Baroque and Latin American Fiction.* University of Chicago Press, 2006.
———. *Magical Realism: Theory, History, Community*. Edited by Lois Parkinson Zamora and Wendy B. Faris. Durham: Duke University Press, 1995.

Chapter Seven

Cuban Theater and the Environmental Dilemma

Karina Pino Gallardo,
Translated by Emmanuel A. Pardo

When looking at recent years, it is possible to recognize gestures and diverse intentions pointing to a rethinking of the relationship between theater and environment in the landscape of the Cuban theater scene. They are mainly fueled by anguish: how to represent the impact of existing strategies of erosion in the contemporary world and the need to preserve the natural balance between humankind and its environment? How does one show, through theater, an art where representation before a spectator defines a certain quality of unreality, the real pain for the loss of that essential balance, the complex relationship between humans and their habitat, death, or gradual deterioration of a system of links between beings, natural phenomena, and spaces whose formation and survival has taken millions of years?

In the Cuban context, we would have to consider certain factors when analyzing this relationship, such as the scarce industrialization of the country as part of that strange "strip" of nations called Third World, and its socialist system of government, which led to the existence of environmental policies and naturally less aggressive forms of natural exploitation. This brings up another important element in the field of Cuban theater, at least in the one developed after 1959, when the artistic sphere entered a phase of intense strengthening: there are not many examples of groups, projects, and artists who have been willing to dedicate their work to exploring the impact of climate change and its causes originating in human action, the erosion of ecosystems, pollution, and the disappearance of entire species.

It is possible to find, however, efforts produced within community-based projects, such as works of Escambray Theater, founded in the 1970s, and many of the works performed by Teatro de los Elementos and its director Jose Oriol González. Moreover, important scripts and performances were developed in the 1970s and 1980s. In those decades, the country still supported cultural strategies that allowed theater artists to address concerns of political, social, and racial topics through their art. The concept of the marginal, the contradictions born of a new sociopolitical system, which generated strong strains and was still immersed in the battle to find a stable path of development, were also present in this period. Then in the 1990s, most of the projects that emerged under the birth of the National Council for the Performing Arts (1989) had to struggle for survival at a critical moment where, in addition to economic shocks that marked one of the most remarkable periods of economic crisis in the history of Cuba, issues such as emigration and family divisions became evident. This also meant the breakdown of a social utopia that had hitherto sustained the hope of several generations of Cubans who remained in the country.

All these elements worked to characterize a theater community dedicated to understanding and exploring, from a thematic point of view, what was happening in Cuba. Paradoxically, they helped to develop the search for new expressive languages and poetics of authorship related to avant-garde influences by international referents that began entering the country starting in the 1980s. Thus, the turbulent and changing political, social, and cultural situation that Cuban citizens and artists experienced well into the 1990s had interests deeply rooted in these elements, which also spanned the ancient preoccupation with the concept of identity and the notion of the Cuban.

The concern with addressing environmental problems has been closely linked to a type of theater that defends the idea of community, the notion of collective creation and work based on experience. The influence of these three points generates an art of procedural nature, where the interest in presenting the theme is powerfully united to an approach to creation that comes from the personal experiences of the artists and their immediate environment. This interest also comes from a way of thinking that, even when it has institutional connections, departs from the original frameworks of traditional production and calls to the power of the individual, to a condition originating from art in relation to nature and in man in relation to the collective.

Thus, there have been projects addressing the topic of environmental protection and the grave danger in which human beings have put themselves in thanks to indiscriminate practices of natural exploitation, but they have done it without a politicized discourse and starting from an essential need: to show certain phenomena occurring in their communities by the power of individual experience, the corporeality of the actor, the performer, and the use of material and cultural elements directly linked to the lives of these men and their communities. We could say that there is virtually no construction, no artificial preparation of the scenery, the costumes, the design of the characters or creatures that the performers embody. There is no ornate construction of the topic, the way the performances are presented to the public, or how the artists conceive of theatrical intervention. There is, though, a communal and individual commitment that is also understood and shared by the community. This is possible thanks to sustained work with the members of such communities, so trained in the reception of this kind of artistic proposals that the majority of times they are integrated into a relation of direct participation.

In recent years, some theater groups have implemented these kinds of strategies in the spaces where they reside. They all work explicitly on environmental topics. On a recent trip, the author of these pages has had the opportunity to share and exchange viewing experiences with American university professors Melinda Levin, Filip Celander, and David Taylor. As part of this collaboration, it was possible to identify some of these groups and projects, all of which were closely connected with the experience of collective creation already rooted in Latin American theater groups since four decades earlier. For example, the work of Jose Oriol González has been influenced by previous experiences such as the *Escambray* and *La Yaya*, who not only conceived their plays based on natural spaces, but also set them in that particular kind of setting. Furthermore, they gave the Cuban peasant, its primary audience, the ability to interact directly and even decide on the fate of the characters and the outcome of such works.

In that case, the history of Teatro de los Elementos is paradigmatic, because it is a collective formed by artists of heterogeneous origin who decided to have not only the experience of working for a community starting from their most urgent conflicts, integrating it and involving it in its efforts, but also because they decided to live in the community and remain in direct relationship with the environment. The land and living space for Teatro de los Elementos can be described as a preserved natural space. Built by its members, it includes spaces for performance such as an amphitheater, and endless possibilities for the engagement of the natural space. In the bridges, rivers, trees, and hills of its land, the group has managed to fuse an interest in including a kind of collective community experience with the environmental problems stemming from that same relationship between man and the environment. The members of Teatro de los Elementos practice and encourage a type of life practice which is not abusive to the local landscape and is interested in dealing with any public environmental problems, whether it is pollution or the drying of a river, water scarcity or the urgent need for its conservation. What matters is how the subject, far from subjugating the formal aspect, integrates with the way the problem is represented, and the group then takes the art of "Playback Theatre" to achieve not only a real and direct communication with the audience, but also a personal exposure of the actors as individuals, who perform without assuming any artifice. The technique allows the public to propose a passage or topic, and the performers to improvise and elaborate with the help of the viewer. The viewer from the community becomes a director, capable of intervening in the presentation of a problem and deciding on the actions of the actor. This collective act radicalizes the estranged relationship which has traditionally owned the stage space and opposed it to the space of the audience, and serves as a powerful area for the confluence of interests, a space for public political exchange in the Ancient Greek sense, a space for unanimous exposition and discussion. The exploration of the theme of environmental conservation is then assumed to be living experience, understood as a circumstance defined by immediacy, and in which it is possible to identify each one of the participants as parts of a community that enjoys and suffers the same tensions and gaps.

The performative dimension of theater, which articulates the moment of scenic representation as a unique situation where certain relationships that are impossible to record or even grasp are produced, defines a special relationship between theater and reality, and enables the generation of a spontaneous and authentic way of addressing topics that would otherwise reach the public turned into pamphlet.

In one of his most seductive works, Spanish professor and theoretician José Antonio Sánchez states, "Reality is the others, real is the relationship itself. The real is immaterial, and it is only representable as a process." The ability to not only generate this process authentically, but also show it through a representational scheme that can materialize issues like the environmental dilemma and the place humans occupy in it, is an important and remarkable achievement, particularly when thinking about the links between theater and reality and between modern humans and their most pressing contradictions.

The work of other groups and projects working in the mountains, in the fields, and inside rural communities can be understood in connection with that same conception. Experiences like those products of the Guantánamo-Baracoa Theater Crusade (Cruzada Teatral Guantánamo-Baracoa), an event conducted annually when various groups in the country visit small villages and hamlets of eastern Cuba for several weeks, create a type of performance art that supports a conception of theater that is more experiential and closer to the social problems affecting this population, among which, of course, there is the relationship of these communities with their environment, with the consequences of severe droughts, and the contamination of the widest rivers in Cuba, the impact of industrialization and the extraction of copper and nickel, and a growing wave of invasive tourism the local population is having to learn to live with.

In such proposals, working with the experiential reflects a commitment that goes beyond aesthetic frameworks, and reaches, in other cases, a more rigorous degree of formal elaboration. This applies, for example, to projects such as *Watermark*, by the group Teatro de la Fortaleza, based in the province of Cienfuegos, and to works by the TECMA project (Theatre Collaboration Environment) in the city of Pinar del Río. Both reside in cities far from the main theater circuits, and both practice experiences of theater in and for the community in which they are part of. They do it using various genres and techniques: the form of theater called dramatic, produced in a theatrical space conditioned by the members of the group Cienfuegos, and street theater, whose impact is also recordable from the number of people who spontaneously join the group in each of its interventions and the relationship it builds with the space in which it operates.

In *Marca de Agua* (*Watermark)* and *Galápago* (*Terrapin*), Atilio Caballero, novelist, poet and playwright, leader of Teatro de la Fortaleza, and Luis Manuel Valdes, director of TECMA, reflect a concern for the development of speech that adds another path to the development of a relationship between theater and environmental reality. Ecological and conservationist thought moves and reaches the viewer through a process of collective creation that leads to a product less influenced by improvisation and public participation in site, instead operating through a more intellectualized and associative reception and building from heterogeneous symbols and references.

Marca de Agua is the result of an experience of research on an extreme situation lived by a city founded in the 1970s, which seems to have been conceived as a space of utopia and realization of the socialist dream. The Ciudad Electronuclear (Nuclear City) (CEN) is located at the foot of the secluded shores of Cienfuegos Bay, and was founded with the construction of three of the five nuclear reactors that would turn the city of Cienfuegos into the mecca of nuclear power generation in Cuba, and where hundreds of engineers would work and live with their families in buildings that were never completed. In the 1990s, the place became a forgotten symbol of a broken utopia. Today, the lives of its inhabitants are full of contradictions with the environment, and the arrival of water in the area, as well as the means to find it, are problems of greater severity. In response, two actors and the director of the group built a creative process that sought to address the issue through dance, the intervention of official documents pertaining to the Kyoto Protocol, and images of the devastation of a city already lost in time. All of this filtered through a markedly poetic language with clear metaphorical undertones and was greatly empowered by the weight of symbols. The product of this work generated discussions that brought to the fore the urgency of a matter made apparent by the body of the actor and the relationship developed with the spectator through a shared experience. Again, the theater serves as a forum and as a site that is political in nature.

Through proposals that erect the performative condition of theater and that radicalize it in connection with a particular community, the approaches to the environmental dilemma and the relevant change produced in the biosphere through years of irresponsible exploitation and depletion of natural resources can finally reach the Cuban viewer, especially in remote towns of the capital and major cities. They establish a more direct relationship with the natural environment and thus perceive more clearly the gradual impact of global policies that have helped damage a delicate natural balance.

Given the limited levels of education and knowledge concerning the environmental dilemma that still affects the contemporary world, a form of art such as theater constitutes an attempt to find answers through a diverse exploration of the concept of experience, of the procedural and the collective. Possibly, the mechanisms of traditional representation would be less efficient because they would create a distance with a spectator deeply in need of developing conscious thinking about the problem. The directors do not put their stakes in fiction, at least not in absolute fiction. Individual and community experience in Cuba has become the fundamental tool to find an answer to the stark choice offered by theater and its relation to reality.

Chapter Eight

Among the Ruins of Ecological Thought

Parasites, Trash, and Nuclear Imaginings in La fiesta vigilada

Christina Maria Garcia

INTRODUCTION

In 2009 additions were made to Havana's topography in the form of two massive installations. Made of steel, an outline of Camilo Cienfuegos's youthful and handsome face was fitted over an exterior wall of the Ministerio de Informática y las Comunicaciones.[1] With his iconic beard and brimmed hat, the national hero's silhouette now accompanies that of Che Guevara's in the Plaza de la Revolución. Measuring forty by thirty-six meters, the monument designed by Enrique Avila required the assistance of a team of workers and cranes. A few months earlier, about five kilometers away in Havana's historic district, a similar scene of coordinated efforts in the mounting of a large installation was visible to the city. For that year's Havana Art Biennial, Roberto Fabelo designed a piece in which giant bronze sculptures of roaches displaying human heads appear to be crawling up the wall of the Museo Nacional de Bellas Artes.[2]

These monumental works, affixed to the facades of institutional buildings, signal diverging imaginaries of past and future histories. Images of Camilo and Che are ubiquitous throughout the country's landscape. They are the icons of the Revolution's vision for a New Man, models of a national subjectivity that is heroic and sacrificial.[3] We might take the steel outlines of these historical figures, agents of a modernizing project, as representing human exceptionalism and the promise of continued future progress, "ever onward to victory" [*hasta la victoria siempre*], as the script below Che's monument reads.[4] If the sculptures in the Plaza de la Revolution are meant to inspire admiration and homage in an uncomplicated commemoration of the past, Fabelo's hybrid creatures, scurrying the walls of the Museo Nacional with their delicate antennas and spindly legs, express an ambivalence toward the future, inspiring both repulsion and fascination. Considering that roaches are believed to be the only creatures to survive a nuclear war or the effects of prolonged pollution, Fabelo's mutant roach-men evoke impeding environmental catastrophe.[5]

Entitled *Survivors* [*Sobrevivientes*], the installation, Fabelo explains, is a "reference to today's world where man in some form or another is surviving" ("Montajes de Sobrevivientes"). In a previous essay on Fabelo's work, I suggested that one way to approximate his designation of "today's world" and the installation's allusion to a disaster yet-to-come is through Gaby Schwab's notion of a "haunting from the future," as we live in the shadow of nuclear object's future effects.[6] I also suggested that the indeterminacy of the piece—Is it a de- or re-humanization? Are the roach-men escaping or invading?—solicits a simultaneous attraction to the biomorphic potential of the insect and its ability to survive, as well as an anxiety regarding ecological concerns.[7] Not incidentally, the indeterminism of Fabelo's installation, its potential for both attraction and anxiety toward nonhuman becomings, and its reference to survival are recurring themes in contemporary cultural production from the island.[8] In her book *Cuban Currency*, Esther Whitfield observes that much of the Cuban state's rhetoric, following the loss of Soviet subsidies during the Special Period in Time of Peace (early to mid-1990s), relied on evoking threats of the Cold War era and the Missile Crisis to garner legitimacy as it failed to provide its citizens with basic needs (143). It is not surprising, then, to find allusions to the effects of an atomic holocaust and more generally to the theme of survival in literary and artistic production. One such example is Antonio José Ponte's 2007 novel, *La fiesta vigilada* , in which he attends to the rubble and ruins of Havana's urban landscape. Linked to these architectural ruins, we also find the ruination of subjectivities deemed unproductive to the Revolution's teleological project. Where monuments such as Camilo's and Che's represent a narrative of progress and victory, Ponte's novel traces the waste left behind by the incessant drive toward a future and the desire to cultivate "a scientific education necessary for the domination of available resources" [*la educación científica necesaria para dominar los recursos disponible*] (187, 188). This call for a "scientific education" by a bureaucrat in the novel is posed against what he conceives as an "erotic" and, therefore, inoperative aesthetic. Ponte's novel, as readers have noted, is explicitly concerned with assigning culpability to the Cuban state for allowing the perpetuation of inhospitable living conditions; a city in ruins, after all, supports the rhetoric of a country under siege (Whitfield, 143;

Silva, 76). That said, in its attention to Havana's inhabited ruins, the novel also illustrates networks of material and territorial interdependencies that exceed the limits of state politics. In the pages that follow, I will underscore these networks through close readings, with the aim of bringing to the foreground an ecological thinking in Ponte's novel, as it challenges the instrumental logic of modernizing projects and displaces the centrality of the human as the agent of history—projects and agents not unlike those invoked in the monuments to Camilo and Che. In *La fiesta vigilada* buildings and trash are anthropomorphized and the inhabitants of Havana's seemingly war-torn buildings appear at moments as parasites, insects, and even algae; they are survivors of an incoming implosion. While numerous insightful readings have been made on *La fiesta vigilada*, particularly with regard to the trope of ruins, Ponte's text has yet to be considered through an ecocritical lens.[9] In adopting such a lens, I not only hope to contribute to the literary criticism on this seminal novel but also, and perhaps more importantly, in thinking with Ponte, to unsettle categorical frames and models of subjectivity that have justified the disposability of different life-forms. Returning to Fabelo's roaches at the end, I will consider how Ponte's ruins and its parasitic survivors express a similar indeterminacy and ambivalence, partaking of an imaginary haunted by the future (Schwab).

UNPRODUCTIVE AND DE/COMPOSING BODIES

"'Pee!', I yelled at her, seeing that she was falling asleep on the toilet. (One evening I cornered her with a broom in the same way one handles rats.) The nights were spent in that tango and in the end it was sweet to hear her urinate" [*'¡Mea!', llegué a gritarle viendo que se dormía en el inodoro. [. . .] Las noches se iban en ese tango y al final era dulce escucharla orinar*]; this Ponte's narrator tells us about his maternal grandmother early in *La fiesta vigilada* (31). Wedged between stories of literary enemies, the fall of the Soviet empire, the Eiffel Tower, and a statue of John Lennon sitting on one of Havana's park benches, we have the deteriorated body of an old senile woman, a body with the "consistency of a rag doll" [*consistencia de muñeca de trapo*] (31). In what turns out to be very infrequent in this novel, Ponte takes some eight uninterrupted pages to narrate an intimate and biographical story, a story, moreover, about incontinence and fragility.

As the first person narrator, the unnamed author recounts his suspension from the Cuban writer's union, UNEAC. With the loss of his civic identity, expulsed from the "lettered city," he wanders through Havana's ruins like a "phantom" (40–47). Yet, the narrator rarely appears as a character in what would seem to be an autobiographical account.[10] With the exception of his voice and parenthetical digressions, he disappears for parts of the narration, as though exiled from his own text, or perhaps transformed into a ghost. The very idea of one's own proper text is called into question when we note the "novel" is composed of a series of retold movie plots, spy fiction, historical events, journalistic information, scholarly essays, topographies, and personal reflections. In short, *La fiesta* reads like a catalogue or a work of assemblage. Its pages are marked by an excessive use of parenthesis, as the narrator appears to slip in wherever he can, producing fissures and ruptures, parasitically. Novelistic conventions such as plot and character development—climactic and voyeuristic devices to lure its readers inside—are largely disused and, instead, Ponte draws his readers outside the text, situating *La fiesta* within a web of other archives, artifacts, and contexts. This is a text without a well-formed body, without a recognizable structure, and among the rubble of other stories, as I aim to demonstrate, we find a pulsating subterranean life, an insistence on corporeality, exposure, and survival.

Before taking a closer look at this life underneath, let us consider the following: The Cuban Revolution "domesticates time" [*doma el tiempo*] (120), states Ponte's narrator; it institutionalizes "what was open adventure" [*lo que fuera aventura abierta*] (121). Shortly after the Revolution's triumph in 1959, leisure, laziness, festivity for the sake of festivity—otherwise considered "killing time while the fields of sugar cane needed cutting" [*mata(r) el tiempo en tanto los campos de caña de azucar necesitaban macheteros*]—became a criminal offence (66, 126). Unproductive expenditure, to use George Bataille's phrase, was closely surveilled and each year was inaugurated with a mission: "Year of Agrarian Reform," "Year of Education," "Year of Planning." After exhausting specific missions, the years were simply commemorated as "Year Thirty of the Revolution" (121). Cabarets and beaches were closed so that time and energy could be spent on not just the fields but, especially, missiles and radars (66). With the advent of the 1962 Missile Crisis, "Havana was declared a battlefield that would last for decades" [*La Habana fue declarada campo de guerra que duraría décadas*], eventually becoming "a Cold War theme park" [*parque temático de la Guerra Fría*] (66, 67). According to our narrator, the revolutionary project was totalizing and, consequently, exclusionary. Invoking Fidel's famous 1961 speech to intellectuals, he writes, "Inside the revolution, everything. But who managed to be inside?" [*Dentro la revolución, todo. Pero ¿quién conseguía estar adentro*?] (122). The all-inclusiveness of Castro's original phrase, "Inside the Revolution, everything; against the Revolution, nothing" [*Dentro de la Revolución, todo; contra la Revolución, nada*], produces a grammar where what is not recognized as contributing the aims of the Revolution is deemed valueless, "nada," and therefore disposable. Put otherwise, its all-or-nothing logic demanded absolute devotion.

Citing the protagonist from Graham Greene's novel *Our Man in Havana*, the narrator states, "faced with the apocalypse Wormold had an epiphany:

'the cruel come and go like cities and thrones and powers, leaving behind their ruins'" [*a Wormold tocaba cierta epifanía frente al apocalipsis*] (Ponte, 65). While the threat of the Missile Crisis in the form of spectacular nuclear bombs never came to be realized, its promise of ruins did in a politics of perpetual antagonisms and slow violence.[11] Wormold's epiphany, regarding the powerful and what they leave behind, might be likened to what Brad Evans and Henry A. Giroux theorize in their book, *Disposable Futures*. Following Zygmunt Bauman, they write:

> Rather than seeing waste as politically useless, Bauman affirms that the production of wasted lives shores up the productivity of the whole system, as the very idea of progress requires the setting aside of those who don't or are unable to perform in a way that would appear meaningful. Criminalization [. . .] performs a vital task by providing scapegoats [. . .] such scapegoats offer an "easy target for unloading anxieties prompted by the widespread fears of social redundancy." [. . .] [T]he incessant drive to progress justifies a form of societal assay that allows for the casting aside of people [for] their own failure to have resources worth extracting. (45, 46)

Although Evans and Giroux's analysis is largely based in contemporary capitalist economies, Cuba's 1971 law against vagrancy and its 1960's labor camps, *Unidades Militares de Ayuda a la Producción*, designed to rehabilitate homosexuals, religious believers, and those deemed antisocial (*Improper Conduct*) are examples of this criminalization and casting aside. Adding to Evans and Giroux's insights on the production of wasted lives, it is useful to recall Bataille's ecological theorization of excess energy in his work *The Accursed Share*. Observing that living organisms ordinarily receive "more energy than is necessary for maintaining life," he argues that this excess should be spent luxuriously and unproductively; otherwise, the outcome will be catastrophic (Bataille, 21). "Humanity exploits given material resources, but by restricting them as it does to a resolution of the immediate difficulties it encounters (a resolution which it has hastily had to define as an ideal), it assigns to the forces it employs an end which they cannot have" (21). To prevent a destructive and ruinous outpouring of energy, Bataille calls for a "general economy"—where transactions are considered within a larger framework that allows for expenditure without gain—against the instrumentality and productiveness of a "restricted economy." In other words, the "erotic" aesthetic the bureaucrat in *La fiesta* complains against (cited in the introduction) and the unpurposive festivities the state aimed to prohibit are not only "inescapable" according to Bataille, but serve an ethical function, allowing for a dissipation of energy before its manifests itself violently (25–26). As though expressing this inevitable dissipation, in one of the novel's parenthetical, sardonic asides, we read that in 1971, assigned "The Year of Productivity," "There were more parasites and lazy people in the country than in all of nineteenth century Russian novels" [*En el país había más parásitos y gente ociosa en toda la novelística rusa del siglo XIX.*] (Ponte, 127).

The casting aside of people that Evans and Giroux observe is operative in *La fiesta* in various ways. Following the verbal news of his suspension from the writers' union, the narrator is unable to recover any documents that would evidence his expulsion and censorship: "My stage as a phantom started without any evidence. [. . .] The order, the official document, the paper, did not exist" [*Mi etapa de fantasma comenzaba sin prueba alguna. [. . .] La orden, el documento oficial, el papel, no existía*] (Ponte, 46). Juxtaposed to passages on the erasure of political identity and "civil death" (33), Ponte narrates intimate, banal, and pathetic scenes in an imperturbable manner. In a less obvious instance of casting away, we learn about the decision to place his grandmother in a state asylum. "Locked up when there was no education left for her, when she was no longer able to adapt herself to new things" [*Encerrada cuando ya no cabía educación para ella, cuando no podia adaptarse a nada nuevo*] (30, 31). At the asylum:

> The bowel movements were cleaned at dawn; the day began with the bathing of the bodies and the boiling of the bedding. (I imagine the clusters of bodies in the despair of insomnia, the urine spreading along the esplanade of those beds united, the stench of the old women.) And during one of her visits my mother found marks of physical harm on the skin of her mother.
>
> [*Las deposiciones eran limpiadas al amanecer, el día comenzaba con el baño de los cuerpos y la hervidura de la ropa de cama. [. . .] Y en una de sus visitas mi mama encontró marcas de golpes en la piel de su mama.*] (Ponte, 31).

In depicting the indignity these incapacitated figures endure, in choosing the word "bodies" instead of "individuals," and in occupying the foreground of the narrative with biological needs, Ponte underscores a bare life. Whereas the discursive boundaries of civic and national identities are considered stable markers of differentiation, immune to changing environments; bodies, as illustrated here, are exposed, contagious, and vulnerable, always in relation to and, at times, indistinguishable from other bodies. The narrator and his mother eventually bring the grandmother back home. Under institutional care she had ultimately been abandoned, exposed to violence and theft (Ponte, 30). Through her bruised skin and defenseless body, unable to even shout, [*no alcanza a la defensa ni al grito*] (31), Ponte conveys an image of absolute dependence.

This foregrounding of corporeality is consistent throughout the text. We are reminded that like the leather produced from a cow's skin, the skin of a man also serves to line material goods: "History could be as cyclical and terrible as that cigarette case lined by human skin assured" [*La historia podría ser tan cicla y terrible como lo aseguraban la cigarrera forrada de piel humana*] (Ponte, 65). Yet the narrator notes that in particular historical accounts "something more underneath appeared to exist [. . .] Notes of color [. . .] seemingly inessential phrases" [*algo más de fondo parecía de existir* [. . .] *Notas de color* [. . .] *frases al parecer inesenciales*] (65, 66). The city itself is described as a mortal body: "so many power cuts like the scars on the forearms of a suicide victim obsessed with the idea of getting closer to the end" [*tantos cortes como cicatrices puedan contener los antebrazos de un suicida obsesionado con la idea de acercarse cada vez más al final*] (71). "The Cuban capital is driven towards implosion, it beats in systole and systole" [*La capital cubana se anima a implosión, late en sístole y sístole*] (174). "Ruins are tortured architecture" [*las ruinas son arquitectura torturada*] (203). With respect to the pages of a text whose errors were marked in red, the narrator tells us it appeared to have "blood ink" [*tinta en sangre*] (48). With this sample of citations, I mean to underscore an insistence on a shared and irreducible corporeality, be that between humans, animals, buildings, and the pages of a text. Ponte, furthermore, animates through this enfleshment what would otherwise be considered inert material sources, or simply a repository of history with no vitality of its own. We might consider the "notes of color" and "inessential phrases" the narrator points to, as that which cannot be subsumed, made a work of, or used as a means to an end. Against the Revolution's taming of time and its narrative of futurity, "something more underneath appeared to exist" (65, 66). I want to note, a shared corporeality, in contrast to an identity, is necessarily improper, it belongs to no one; the phrases "my body," "my text," "my city" could never fully encompass their referents. Accordingly, to treat a shared corporeality, or a cosubstantiality, in an instrumental and compartmentalized manner, as though it was distinct and reducible to a property, will have destructive consequences.[12]

In the novel's depiction of the Revolution's handling of prostitution and gambling we see the negative impacts of treating something in an isolated manner. Ponte illustrates how the state's mission to exterminate what it perceived as immoral and decadent failed to recognize a larger system, an ecology of which slot machines and pimps are only some of its perceptible effects. Instead of addressing poverty and unemployment, cabarets and casinos were closed leaving sex workers and gamblers to find more illicit and precarious venues (Ponte, 81). During the Special Period, prostitution as a mode of survival returned with a vengeance. Curiously, Ponte describes it as an almost inoperative economy, or one whose transactions cannot be measured by monetary gain. Willing to work in exchange for the pleasure of a cold beer, the comfort of a couch, or the simulation of personal affect confused the distinctions between necessity and desire (73). Alternatively, the inefficiency of this prostitution according to a restricted economy, the unproductive expenditure in the fulfillment of a desire for a cold beer, might be considered an inescapable, and necessary, outpouring of excess energy. Resources, as Bataille argues, cannot be reduced to the ends we assign them.

INHABITED RUINS

The distinctions between what is proper and improper, or private and public, are further obscured when we consider the inhabited ruins (Ponte, 167, 168). The collapse between interiority and exteriority, as facades crumble, makes it difficult to determine the boundaries of these buildings. Their porosity and precariousness intensifies their relationship with their surroundings. Just as a body harbors other organisms like bacteria and microbes, the ruins are described as inhabited by parasitic dwellers. Ponte observes that while Havana does not expand its vertical or horizontal limits, the city grows from the inside (174). With the migration of easterners to the capital, expanding families, a housing shortage, and the collapse of other buildings, Havana's inhabitants or dwellers [*moradores*] build walls, divisions, and lofts within existing structures (174). Notably, Ponte hardly, if ever, uses the word residents or individuals, heightening the image of the city as a habitat and ecosystem. The proliferating smaller spaces are often described as corners, hideouts, or closets [*rincón, covacha*] (174). Even rooftops are converted into tiny rooms for which "one didn't know if it was humans or pigeons that should be accredited" [*no se sabría si adjudicar a humanos o palomas*] (174). While these inhabitants carve out spaces for themselves within these structures, chipping away at the buildings' foundations, they are also the ones to consistently repair its damaged roofs, patch surfaces, and drain rainwater (148). In this continuous process of damaging and repairing, the inhabitants appear as integral parts of the buildings; they both animate the buildings and are a source of its destruction (174).[13]

Citing a Spanish essayist on the stages of ruination, the narrator writes, "The vegetal carrion appear during the last act. 'There is no ruin without plant life, without ivy, moss or jaramago that sprouts in the crack of the stone, confused with the lizard, as a delirium of life born of death,' said Maria Zambrano" [*Durante el último acto aparecían los vegetales carroñeros. "No hay ruina sin vida vegetal; [. . .] como un delirio de la vida que nace de la muerte," determino María Zambrano"*] (Ponte, 164). The cyclical link between "life" and "death," the emergence of vegetation from within a crack, and the assimilation of its greenery to that of a reptile is, perhaps, a classic image of the persistence and indistinction of "nature." What is not however classic is the assimilation of human reproduction, or filial expansion, to that of proliferating plant life: "The vegetal [. . .] begins with a tree inside the house, the genealogical one" [*Lo vegetal* [. . .] *comienza por un árbol dentro de la casa, el genalógico*] (175). In the poetics of this novel, human figures often cross into a zone of biological organisms, exhibiting qualities of rodents, insects, and even algae. The inhabitants of ruins are described as "scurrying" [*escabullían*] (148). At another point, they emerge from a power outage drawn to the bright windows of a hotel, like moths to a light. These illuminated panes of glass appear as "fish tanks" in the dark of night [*la gente* [. . .] *emergía del apagón para acercarse a esas peceras*] (72). In a passage referring to the state's response to an epidemic we read, "Faced with the fumigations that made the interior of the domiciles unbreathable, also we, inhabitants, exited on to the street" [*En vista de que las fumigaciones volvían irrespirable el interior de los domicilios, también nosotros, moradores, salíamos a la calle*] (145). With that "also we," Ponte's narrator implicitly situates himself and his neighbors alongside that which needed to be disinfected and purged; as part of the same environment they are also vulnerable to the fumes. In a phrase that expresses the height of abjection, we read: "The state shelters house a stratum of humans as slimy as that which covers standing water" [*los albergues estatales guardan una capa humana tan legamosa como lo que cubre las aguas estancadas*] (175).

People are not the only ones to adopt other ontologies. In the rapid deterioration of buildings in Cuba, we can observe processes of change in materials conventionally perceived as solid and stable. As suggested in the section on corporeality, materials in *La fiesta* are charged with a vitality of their own. In Ponte's grammar, objects, such as a potted plant, a fan, or the Eiffel Tower, occupy the position of subject; they are agents of action (28, 91, 15). The presumably inanimate are also depicted as the recipients of emotional injuries: "he insulted her" [*la insultó*], the pronoun her standing in for the Eiffel Tower (15). In the following passage we see how an architectural structure fought with its last breath to stay alive, so to speak:

> [T]he ancient hotel Pasaje resisted the disequilibrium they caused him. Life appeared to continue the same for one night and the half of a morning. Until the structure could no longer stand it, he released a whistle, a stream of dust to the sky, and fell down.
>
> [*el antiguo hotel Pasaje resistió el desequilibrio que le causaran.* [. . .] *y se vino abajo.*] (Ponte, 161)

That particles of dust should produce a stream [*un chorro de polvo*], transforming solid into liquid matter, is another example of how Ponte's poetics unsettle ontological categories. Illustrating the complex and delicate networks of which this structure is a part, heightened in its precarious state, the narrator surmises, in his characteristic parenthetical asides, "(The final straw could have been the closing of a door, someone who closed a refrigerator after serving themselves water)"[*(El colmo pudo ser el cierre de una puerta, alguien que cerraba un refrigerador luego de servirse agua)*] (161).

Recalling George Simmel's writings on ruins, the narrator explains that the German philosopher found inhabited ruins disquieting and blamed its inhabitants for abetting nature, a force they should have banded against (Ponte, 165). For Simmel, ruins—that is, those not too demolished that their original form is imperceptible, and certainly not ones with people living in them—afforded the contemplation of nature's vengeance over culture's transcendental spirit. But to appreciate this dialectical relationship, these two antagonizing forces must remain distinct. The inhabitants of ruins, complicit with nature, collapse this distinction; "they betrayed man and demonstrated how little soul they had" [*traicionaban a los hombres y demostraban cuán poca alma tenían*] (Ponte, 166). What, then, might be gained or revealed from a sustained attention to Havana's ruins, a zone of indistinction, and abject living conditions?

As a self-identified ruinologist, Ponte's narrator expresses ambivalence toward his trade. He acknowledges that in representing Havana's ruins, in perpetuating this particular trope, he, inadvertently, not only contributes to an ongoing process of the city's museumification and its image as a Cold War theme park, but also supports the state's narrative of a permanent state of emergency (205–39). However, as Whitfield demonstrates in her reading of *La fiesta* and other works by Ponte, these ruins in their very persistence are also for him a source of hope. She explains,

> For Simmel, the people whom he saw living in Roman ruins were unambiguously agents of those ruins' destruction, parasites who could only weaken their host's structure and power to charm. Their very presence broke the spell of silence that surrounds a ruin proving them to be complicit with, as Ponte puts it, "one of the two adversaries," the one charged with destruction. [. . .] [T]he squatters had to be nature's accomplices. And yet, to what Simmel laments as the dilapidation of an aesthetic affect, Ponte opposes a hope that the buildings, and thence the life within them, will remain standing against the odds. [. . .] Rather than mere accomplices in the destruction of their dwellings, Ponte suggests, might not these survivors be double agents, in the service of both decay and hope? (Whitfield, 144)

The imagined dichotomy that Simmel wants to guard between nature and culture buttresses the notion of human exceptionalism and its teleological projects. These modernizing and utopic projects, let us remember, have roots in Enlightenment rubrics and have relied on an instrumental and compartmentalizing logic to justify processes of exploitation and casting aside.[14] I want to suggest that in breaking the spell, in obstructing the distanced contemplation of "culture" and "nature," the inhabited ruins do *not* allow us to disavow a shared materiality with our environment; the inhabited ruins make evident that we are always in a relationship of interdependence.

While Ponte is certainly invested in exposing a system of censorship and social death—a mode of disposing those considered unproductive to the Revolution's ends—we have seen that intertwined with texts, buildings, and the city (all of which are associated with intelligent, discursive life), is the corporeal, the material, and the indistinguishable. In illustrating the simultaneity of being a political phantom, or politically "dead," and being corporeally "alive," the text draws our attention to the persistence of life underneath (or zoē), that which modernizing projects have strived to domesticate through "scientific education," "culture," and "progress." Following Whitfield, it is the very parasitic ability of the dwellers to survive that gives Ponte hope and not, I would add, a reclaiming of national identity or the exhibition of heroic sacrifices.

As I noted at the beginning of the chapter, *La fiesta vigilada* does not provide us with a cohesive structure that would constitute a recognizable literary work. In appropriating other novels, essays, films, and historical events, assembled with seemingly insignificant accounts of invisible lives, Ponte, not unlike the inhabitants of ruins, expresses a symbiotic relationship; he destroys as he constructs, eating away at the integrity of other structures. The novel's lack of biographical information and the space allotted to summaries of other narratives reiterate a sense of impropriety. Inserting digressions and personal reflections between parentheses, the narrator appears to burrow spaces in a structure of which he does not belong. In effect, he produces and inhabits a ruin at the level of the writing. Where one might expect for Ponte to insist on an enduring humanism or the recovery of his civic identity through an edifying work of literature, he, instead, adopts the very techniques of the parasitic dwellers. On the last page of the novel, referring to a museum's guest book, the narrator claims, "I managed to *scurry* away without writing anything in it" [*logré escabullirme sin escribir nada en él*] (Ponte, 239). Such scurrying and slipping away recall Fabelo's roaches on the exterior walls of the Museo Nacional. In place of leaving a legacy, his name for posterity, Ponte's narrator, like the parasitic dwellers, opts for survival. In the same way his narrative strategies emulate their parasitic practices, we might consider the dwellers, in turn, as anonymous writers, who leave their traces and re-create the city from within.[15] Ponte's text is no doubt aimed at exposing "dehumanizing" living conditions, but rather than appeal to a transcendental spirit, he elevates the less-than-human, the discarded, and the useless.

TALKING TRASH

In her reading of Pedro Juan Gutierrez's novels, Whitfield explains how Havana's residential quarters appear as "habitats" animated by the "human beings" who live in them (106, 107). Borrowing a concept from Jane Bennett, I would like to suggest that in *La fiesta vigilada*, Ponte allows us to imagine an ecology where buildings are not simply animated by humans but by their very own "vibrant matter." Indeed, as we have seen, objects in the text are often depicted as having agency and a capacity to feel. In her book, *Vibrant Matter: A Political Ecology of Things*, Bennett aims "to detach materiality from the figures of passive, mechanistic, or divinely infused substance," and argues, "vibrant matter is *not* the raw material for the creative activity of humans or God" (xiii). Echoing Bataille's theory of excess energy and material resources, she observes an "impersonal affectivity" of things that is irreducible to their instrumentality. Her book challenges anthropocentrism and calls for an attentiveness to "the capacity of things—edibles, commodities, storms, metals—not only to impede or block the will and designs of humans but also to act as quasi agents or forces with trajectories, propensities, or tendencies of their own" (Bennett, viii). Early in her text, Bennett describes an encounter with some debris—a dead rat, a white bottle cap, a black plastic glove, and a piece of wood—in the following way:

> [T]hese items shimmered back and forth between debris and [. . .] stuff that commanded attention in its own right, as existents in excess of their association with human meanings, habits, or projects. [. . .] [The] stuff exhibited its thing-power: it issued a call, even if I did not quite understand what it was saying. At the very least, it provoked affects in me. (4)

Ponte offers us a similar scene in *La fiesta vigilada.* Following an epidemic that broke out in a neighborhood due to standing water, there was an official campaign to "throw out all that was useless from homes"; consequently, "accumulated junk started to float outside" [*echar fuera de casa todo lo innservible y comemzaban a salir a flote los tarecos acumulados*] (145). Expressing an affective attachment toward this junk, as well as a parallel between the inhabitants and the discarded, we read "It was hard to say goodbye [. . .] we tied ourselves to the refuse" [C*ostaba dar adios . . . nos amarraba a desecho*s] (145). The passage continues:

> An egg shell, a broken lantern, the sole of a shoe: if they had served us in their useful lives, they should accompany us as remains. [. . .] The stores on Murralla street vomited goods. [. . .] At dawn, Bernaza was carpeted with cards from a board game that never came to be played, a sort of trivial material dialectic. (The wind shuffled the cards now.) [. . .]
>
> "Then all the discarded things that fell silent during the day found voices" wrote Lord Dunsay. Each one in turn, in one of his stories spoke the articles of the garbage dump:
>
> A) a cork grown in the forests of Andalusia,
> B) an unscathed match,

> C) an old and broken teapot, calling herself friend of the cities,
> D) a piece of rope cursed from its origin ("I was made in a place of condemnation, and the condemned knit my fibers in a job without hope. Since then remained the filth of leisure in my heart").
>
> [*Un cascarón de huevo, una linterna rota, la suela despegada de un zapato: [. . .]*
> *D) un pedazo de cuerda maldita desde el origen (<<Fui hecha en un lugar de condena, y condenados tejieron mis fibras en un trabajo sin esperanza. De entonces me quedó la mugre del ocio en el corazón>>].* (145)

In Ponte's characteristic anthropomorphization, the stores "vomited" the material goods, and fibers of a rope have a heart; these fibers, moreover, carry the sentiments of those who made them, "the filth of leisure." Arguably, Ponte is using a literary, allegorical device; however, we should note another theme of the novel: "miraculous static" [*estática milagrosa*]. As a term deployed by "experts" to account for buildings that remained upright against all knowledge of physics (Ponte, 173), "miraculous static" is perhaps, in its mystery to human understanding, akin to "vibrant matter." With this inventory of random objects occupying space in the text and their becoming "remains," or auratic relics, in their very uselessness, Ponte illustrates, like Bataille and Bennett, how material resources exceed the utilitarian ends and even cultural meanings we ascribe to them. Ponte also shows how the "useless" does not go away. It floats on to the street. That which has been deemed trash has a power and affectivity of its own and continues to be a part our environment. Tellingly, the narrator refers to the shuffled game cards as a "trivial material dialectic." Let us recall, historical materialism aims to demystify the fetishistic power of man-made things. Bennett, by contrast, proposes cultivating "a bit of anthropomorphism—the idea that human agency has some echoes in nonhuman nature—[. . .] to counter the narcissistic reflex of human language and thought" (xvi). Bennett's vital materialism and ecological thinking upends the logic that would justify the sacrifice of the "useless" for instrumental ends. To quote her once more,

> Such a newfound attentiveness to matter and its powers will not solve the problem of human exploitation or oppression, but it can inspire a greater sense of the extent to which all bodies are kin in the sense of inextricably enmeshed in a dense network of relations. And in a knotted world of vibrant matter, to harm one section of the web may very well be to harm oneself. (13)

CONCLUSION

Returning to the steel outlines of Camilo's and Che's handsome faces, with which we started, monumentalized for all the city to see, we find the archetypes of a national identity. Interestingly, in her analysis of different aesthetic strategies, Natalia Brizuela notes "nation-building narratives that are themselves based on structures of exclusion, differentiation, and value of particular kinds of ideological identification are enacted through the language and the pathos of the face" (62). The ideological identification, as elaborated in Che's writing, is one of heroism and sacrifice for a providential future.[16] Such calls to sacrifice have at times manifested in the criminalization and disposability of those who did not correspond to the model of a morally and physically incorruptible New Man.[17] Moreover, the historical narrative that is invoked in the memorialization of the Revolution's martyrs is one of sovereignty and human exceptionalism; it is a history grounded on a dialectical logic of clear antagonists, perhaps best epitomized by Cold War politics.

Roberto Fabelo's installation, on the other hand, presents us not with recognizable, historic figures, but with a swarm of roach-men. The hybridity of these creatures evokes a planetary threat, exceeding the discursive limits of the nation-state and a politics of adversaries. Fabelo's statement that the piece is a "reference to today's world" alludes not only to the psychic effects this future catastrophe has on the present moment, but also the material deprivation that such a threat generated. The Special Period in Time of Peace, as Ponte has argued in *La fiesta*, inaugurated a state of exception that demanded from its citizens extraordinary measures in order to survive. While the threat of nuclear war posed by the Missile Crisis did not come to fruition, Havana still bears its wounds and is, at present, surviving. Fabelo and Ponte thus complicate a linear temporality and counter the futurity of the state's rhetoric of sacrifice.

Like Fabelo's roaches, in Ponte's depiction of Havana's inhabited ruins—buildings whose facades (or faces) have crumbled away, exposing delicate networks—we do not find individual heroic figures, but a swarm of survivors. While Ponte assigns culpability to the Cuban state for creating the living conditions in which people have been reduced to a parasitic state of being, at the same time, it is their very parasitic attributes that have allowed them to survive. Ponte's ambivalence leads us to consider the critical question how a literary or visual piece might do the work of protesting "inhuman" or "dehumanizing" conditions while not appealing to a transcendental humanism or resorting to the discourse of human rights. In his treatment of Havana's inhabited ruins, in the language of his poetics, we are brought to imagine forms of relations that bypass and exceed conventional ontological markers; we are brought to imagine the material as having its own transformative potential outside of human agency. Given these dynamic relations, such thinking necessarily acknowledges the impossibility of mastery or of knowing absolutely. The corporeal vulnerability illustrated on both formal and representational registers in *La fiesta vigilada* undermines the presumptions of human sovereignty and calls attention to our material and territorial interdependence.

NOTES

1. See Morejón Rodriguez for pictures and journalistic report on the installation (http://www.cubadebate.cu/fotorreportajes/2009/10/27/camilo-ya-esta-en-la-plaza-de-la-revolucion/#.WccyCtOGNPV).
2. See "Montaje de Sobrevivientes," for a video of Fabelo's installation (https://www.youtube.com/watch?v=ZZVWmzY4sPY).
3. See Guevara. In his vision of the generation to come, "el hombre del futuro" is compelled by heroic duty, knowing that "liberty and its daily maintenance are colored in blood and are full of sacrifice" [*libertad y su sostén cotidiano tienen color de sangre y están henchidos de sacrificio*] (https://www.marxists.org/espanol/guevara/65-socyh.htm#n*).
4. All translations from Spanish to English are mine.
5. See Carton (http://www.fotolibra.com/gallery/533546/giant-mutant-cockroaches-havana).
6. See García and Schwab.
7. In her book, *Metamorphoses: Towards a Materialist Theory of Becoming*, Rosi Braidotti writes, "[Insect life] dwells between different states of in-between-ness, arousing the same spasmodic reactions in humans as the monstrous, the sacred, the alien. This is a reaction of simultaneous attraction and repulsion, disgust and desire. They pose the question of radical otherness not in metaphorical but in bio-morphic terms, that is to say as a metamorphosis of the sensory and cognitive apparatus" (149).
8. For other examples, see Ahmel Echevarría's and Ena Lucía Portela's novels.
9. In addition to Whitfield and Silva, also see Kanzepolsky, Rojas, Romo Carmona, Alvarez Borland, Birkenmaier, Palmero González, and Laddaga, for criticism on the novel.
10. See Kanzepolsky for a reading of how Ponte complicates the conventions of autobiography.
11. "Jean Paul Sartre was not mistaken to conjecture that, had the United States of America not existed, the Cuban revolution would have been invented them. The American proximity (proximity that is danger) is incessantly remembered in the revolutionary speeches. And for such a thought, Havana is less a living city than a landscape of political legitimation" [*Jean Paul Sartre no se equivocó al conjeturar que, de no existir los Estados Unidos de América, la revolución cubana se los habría inventado. La proximidad norteamericana (proximidad que es peligro) es incesantemente recordada en las alocuciones revolucionarias. Y, para un pensamiento así, La Habana es menos ciudad viva que paisaje de legitimación política*] (Ponte, 204).

See Nixon on slow violence. Within the context of Cuba we can point to the debilitating economic constraints imposed by the U.S. embargo and (as per Ponte) the Cuban State's willful neglect to improve living conditions as forms of unspectacular violence. As we'll see further ahead, Ponte's account is also a testament to processes of social death in the form of criminalization, expulsion, and censorship. The above quote speaks to a politics of clearly defined antagonists; such a binary distinction (recalling here Castro's 1971 quote) produces a context of vigilance and policing.

12. On the destructiveness of compartmentalization and mere purposive rationality see Bateson. For the concepts *cosubstantial* and *enfleshment* see Povinelli.
13. In addition to the novel, these processes and relationships are also expressed in Florian Borchmeyer's 2006 documentary, *Arte nuevo de hacer ruinas*, which Ponte narrates. See also Whitfield's description of *solares* in other texts by Pedro Juan Gutiérrez, where she describes them as "animated" by their inhabitants (106).
14. Symptomatic of this compartmentalizing logic, we might recall, in addition to the 1960's forced labor camps (UMAPS), the Cuban state's involuntary quarantines for those infected with HIV in the 1980s. See Mirta Suquet Martínez.
15. I want to thank George Allen for prompting me to consider the relationship between writing and the dwellers of the ruins.
16. See note #1.

17. See note #12, Mirta Suquet Martínez explains how the Cuban Revolution's public health policy (and its corresponding moral codes) manifested itself in the medicalization of the New Man as an immune man (303), and the documentary *Improper Conduct*.

WORKS CITED

Almendros, Néstor, and Orlando Jiménez Leal, directors. *Improper Conduct*. France 2 (FR2), 1984.

Bataille, Georges. *The Accursed Share Volume I*. Translated by Robert Hurley. Zone Books, 1991.

Bateson, Gregory. *Steps to an Ecology of Mind*. Jason Aronson Inc., 1972, 1987.

Bennett, Jane. *Vibrant Matter: A Political Ecology of Things*. Duke University Press, 2009.

Birkenmaier, Anke. "La Habana y sus otros: presencias fantasmagóricas en La fiesta vigilada de Antonio José Ponte y La neblina del ayer de leonardo Padura." In *Cultura y letras cubanas en el siglo XXI*, edited by Araceli Tinajero, 245–60. Iberoamericana, 2010.

Borchmeyer, Florian, director. *Arte nuevo de hacer ruinas*. Gluek Auf film, 2006.

Borland, Isabel Alvarez. "Soy un ciego empeñado en leer blancos: liminaridad y posmemoria en La fiesta vigilada de Antonio José Ponte." *Caribe: revista de cultura y literatura* 13, no. 2 (2010): 111–28.

Braidotti, Rosi. *Metamorphoses: Towards a Materialist Theory of Becoming*. John Wiley & Sons, 2013.

Brizuela, Natalia. "Sense of Place: Paz Encina's Radical Poetics." *Film Quarterly*, vol. 70, no. 4 (2017): 49–64.

Carton, David John. "Giant mutant cockroaches, Havana." http://www.fotolibra.com/gallery/533546/giant-mutant-cockroaches-havana. Accessed May 7, 2015.

Echevarría Peré, Ahmel. *Búfalos camino al matadero*. Editorial Oriente, 2013.

Evans, Brad, and Henry A. Giroux. *Disposable Futures: The Seduction of Violence in the Age of Spectacle*. City Lights Publishers, 2015.

García, Christina. "Incorrect and Beautiful Anatomies: Becomings, Immanence, and Transspecies Bodies in the Art of Roberto Fabelo." In *Re-Encountering Animal Bodies*, edited by Matthew Calarco and Dominik Ohrem. Palgrave Macmillan, forthcoming.

Guevara, Che. "El socialism y el hombre en Cuba." 1965. https://www.marxists.org/espanol/guevara/65-socyh.htm#n*. Accessed May 10, 2015.

Kanzepolsky, Adriana. "¿Yo no soy el tema de mi libro? La fiesta vigilada de Antonio José Ponte." *Abehache*, año 1, no. 1–2 (2011): 59–69.

Laddaga, Reinaldo. "La intimidad mediada: Apuntes a partir de un libro de Antonio José Ponte." *Hispanic review*, vol. 75, no. 4 (2007): 331–48.

"Montaje de Sobrevivientes." *Museo Nacional de Bellas Artes*. 10ma Edición de la Bienal de la Habana, 2009. https://www.youtube.com/watch?v=ZZVWmzY4sPY. Accessed February 10, 2017.

Nixon, Rob. *Slow Violence and the Environmentalism of the Poor*. Harvard University Press, 2011.

Palmero González, Elena C. "El rastro y la ruina: tras la huella de Antonio José Ponte y Abilio Estévez." *Alea: Estudos Neolatinos*, vol. 15, no. 1 (2013): 41–57.

Ponte, Antonio José. *La fiesta vigilada*. Editorial Anagrama, 2007.

Portela, Ena Lucía. *El pájaro: pincel y tinta china*. Editorial Casiopea, S. L., 1998.

Povinelli, Elizabeth A. *Economies of Abandonment: Social Belonging and Endurance in Late Liberalism*. Duke University Press, 2011.

Rodríguez, Morejón. "Camilo ya está en la Plaza de la Revolución." *Cubadebate: Contra el Terrorismo Mediático*, 2009. http://www.cubadebate.cu/fotorreportajes/2009/10/27/camilo-ya-esta-en-la-plaza-de-la-revolucion/#.WccyCtOGNPV. Accessed August 15, 2017.

Rojas, Rafael. "Diaspora, intelectuales y futuros de Cuba." *Temas* 66 (2011): 144–51.

Romo Carmona, Mariana. "No se puede ser cubano en cualquier parte: la metáfora del derrumbe en "La fiesta vigilada" y "Cien botellas en una pared." *Crítica hispánica*, vol. 35, no. 2 (2013): 141–54.

Schwab, Gabriele. "Haunting from the Future: Psychic Life in the Wake of Nuclear Necropolitics." *The Undecidable Unconscious: A Journal of Deconstruction and Psychoanalysis,* vol. 1 (2014): 85–101.

Silva, María Guadalupe. "Antonio José Ponte: el espacio como texto." *Iberoamericana*, año 14, no. 53 (2014): 69–83.

Suquet Martinez, Mirta. *Rostros del VIH/sida. Enfermedad e identidad en las narrativas del yo latinoamericanas: perspectiva comparada.* Dissertation, Universidad de Santiago Compostela, 2016. http://hdl.handle.net/10347/14757. Accessed June 8, 2016.

Whitfield, Esther Katheryn. *Cuban Currency: The Dollar and "Special Period" Fiction.* Vol. 21. University of Minnesota Press, 2008.

Appendix

Literary Responses

Chapter Nine

Of the African in Cuba

Heriberto Feraudy Espino,
Translated by David Taylor

"IBÚ AOKÓ"

There is a tale of Afro-Cuban mythology that there once was a river of deep, clean, and crystalline waters born and raised before time, but it was so presumptuous and arrogant because it was famous for what was written by Heraclitus and others.

Ibú Aokó (white river), which was what the river was called, once heard a discussion about what was said by the celebrated philosopher. Some said that he said, "No one bathes twice in the waters of the same river." Others claimed that he had said, "You cannot bathe twice in the same river."

"Ha ha ha," the river laughed. "I do not know what the presocratic Heraclitus said. I only know that I am the best of the best because the best ewètegbodo (plants) grow on my shores, the best eyá (fish) are born in my waters, and my bottom is fine sand."

Afefe (the wind), as he passed by and heard the claim of the boastful river, said, "That is not enough dear friend."

"Well, if that is not enough, then also know that I am the mirror of Olorun (the sun), Oshupa (the moon), and Irawó (the stars) and even the sea receives me with pleasure to sweeten its salty waters."

"But that's not enough, my dear friend, if you do not have the man's attention," the wind returned.

It turned out that, when in the land of Santa Brava, where Ibú Aokó was born and raised, Ibú Aokó and Afefe came to give power to the wise, they saw written in the sand of the already extensive and deep ibú the following proverb: "Ingratitude is the daughter of arrogance." It was Olofin's message addressed to the men of that land, but the Okurin (men) did not heed the message.

Time passed and with it the spring and with the spring came the rains. The waters of that river began to muddy, the mud of its bottom to stir up. With so much oyuro (rain) that fell, the waters grew, and they left the river channel.

The men of that ará (Earth) did not remember what was said by Olofin, and instead of going to see the Moyé (sages) to know what to do, they only concentrated on other minor tasks.

It was then that Ibú Aokó saw a stream that had been raised by the rains, entering a junction and carrying with it yellowish waters and riots full of dry leaves and clusters of old branches.

The angry river faced the Omodó (stream) and said, "Neither you nor any of your friends are authorized to bring me their dirty and stinking waters, come to disturb me and rob me of my happiness! Get away from me, to marshes and marshes."

Omodó was the son of Oshún, goddess of the sweet waters. Feeling offended and mistreated by the pride of that ibú, he went to give the complaints to his iyá (mother), who decided to order their other children to run to other places. The oyusó (springs) that were brothers of the streams were also offended by Ibú Aokó and decided to take another way.

Soon in the dry river beds were puddles of dirty water and mosquitoes and contaminated piles of rotting leaves; the eweko (plants) and the eyá (fish) dried up. Ibú had no food left. The iléyé (birds) that lived on its waters fled.

The Ibú of Santa Brava became thin. His breath was short, and he felt very cold. He said, "There were things that I used to do before and now I could not do, and the men did nothing."

One day Olokun, whom some consider a man and others, a woman, but without doubt the deity of the sea and the ocean where it is bound by seven chains, asked, "What will have become of that ibú that brought me its sweet waters all the weather?"

Olokun went to see Olofin, and there he met Oshun Iyumo, who said, "Olokun, Ibu Aokólo left the poorly thanked men who did not know how to take care of him properly and so dried up."

Time passed, and a bird passed, and by the ingratitude of the men that town was left without water.

Chapter Ten

The Gardener's Creed

Alison Hawthorne Deming

I walked with friends in Havana
and made an accidental friend—
would you like to see the garden
where Fidel preached to students though
preach may suggest devotion
to one god over the others
when he was secular as I
am believing in rice and corn—
the stranger who became a friend
accompanying us for hours.

He took us to the garden of
laurels on campus where before
the revolution Fidel spoke
from the balcony and below
the students rallied. A bronze stands
at the entrance—formerly school
of biology now math which
seems right when calculus of loss
seems our law of nature—the bronze
Professor Felipe Aloy

Don Felipe to fishermen
who knew him from daily visits
to the market—twenty years' worth—
when the fishes came in from boats
at noon. In 1826
he sailed to Paris carrying
85 drawings of Cuban
fishes and 35 species
stored in a barrel of brandy.

The spirit of discovery

fueled by patience and love.
Friend of the fishermen he worked
in France with Cuvier
and Valenciennes on the
Natural History of the Fishes
(he'd studied snails too and insects
all the unknowns of his time)
thus 782
new fish species from Cuba
were added to the world's wealth.

There's more to learn than names and shapes
and habitats though knowing them
means wanting them to be: trogon
bee-hummingbird polymita
snail and anoles that eat them
hutia croc tree-boa kite
the fishing bat with two-foot wings
egret finch flamingo heron
smallest scorpion in the world.
Each a calibration a calculus

in bone or shell or hide—each
an instrument for telling time
and knowing where they are in space
and savoring whatever form
they land in as they come to life.
Rings on clam shells and inside trees
count each year's passing with detail
on weather and hardships endured.
That's how we know reading fossil
clams and corals that deposit

one ring of lime once each day
how long a day is and how long
a day used to be—puny
400 million years ago
at 22 hours. The moon
has been a drag on Earth's rotation.
I know that numbers are numbing
when what everyone wants to feel
is to feel for life enough not
to waste its future away.

Embargo sanction and blockade
are the language of politics

when it should be yucca guava
sweet potato pollo water
air. No one in Havana was
impressed with our dumbfounding grief
Americans arriving with
our election still stuck in our
throats a cry that could not quite get
past our lips so sure had we been

about loving the idea
we were the virtuosos of
democracy though the raw wounds
of civil war keep playing out
on our streets and Earth beloved
Earth denied in her need and that
was not the story we thought we
lived in we for whom natural
beauty had been a national
creed. When we arrived in Cuba

the week of mourning had ended
Fidel everywhere—photos
lining mahogany shelves where
archeological records
and specimens were on display
Fidel swinging a golf club then
at the Hotel Nationale
standing floor to ceiling between
antique grandfather clocks Fidel
with rifle and khaki knapsack.

People were shocked at how many
mourners amassed to pay tribute.
Sad said the drivers in vintage
cars but mounted on their dashboards
were photos of their cars not Fidel.
They say we're free said our new friend
but we've had 58 years
of control and discipline.
Young people don't want
a revolution. They want nice shoes.

After the Soviets left Cubans
suffered. Rations meant to last
a month—rice chicken sugar salt
sweet potato (list posted on
chalkboard in tiny corner store)—
last a week and who has money?

Military and police. Don't
ask about the writers unless
you want to know silence exile
prison worse. Our translator

struggled with the phrase "world of grief."
Hard to translate. *Añoranza*
he said—yearning longing for
something past. The edens in our
minds always egging us to
plant and grow and weed bending
kneeling down to meet the earth
sitting to contemplate the green
that finds the spaces between stones
and leaves as they unbend slowing

down to watch the sweet potato
vines sprawl beyond the enclosure
of the garden bed—green that finds
a ruin something to root into
for nourishment that finds a fence
something to climb for added strength
that finds the city whatever
ideology has raised it
or allowed it to fall the new
patchwork eden goodness sewn anew.

I believe in gardens. Often
I am permitted to return
to a garden as if it were
(dear Duncan's lines that are not mine
but mined to be the made place that
is mine it is so near the heart)
a stay against the sun going
down a property of mind that
rises out of ruin so tuned
to soil is soul (call it what you will

that stay against oblivion).
Mussels and clams and corals tune
into celestial rhythm
marking each day in a ring of lime.
What cosmic measure do my bones
take of the day and year? Surely
I am as connected to the
spheres as a mollusk. That's why I
count syllables and lines in endless
love with the metrics of connection.

We don't see beyond our pets said
Armando in *commentario*
a lament that we build structures
animals don't understand.
The bear who eats from garbage cans
the coyote who drinks from fountains.
We took the rivers away from them.
Our pets look at us almost asking
what we want from them. They too are
mystified by our power but still

love us. I believe the garden
can sew up wounds in a city.
Words too though words can open wounds
anew. I would rather be a
woman of the corn than one of
asphalt feel the *alisios*
blow through tassels the sea
combing out words tangled in my hair
yucca bilongo paella
santería bolero eolica

Would you like to try a 500-
year-old drink? Yes we told our
accidental friend and walked to
the alley of outsider art
a little shrine for *santería*
sacrifice we'd already seen
a headless rooster lying on
a curb near the police station
Yoruba gods surviving
transplantation to Havana

and in the café where men smoked
montecristos we sipped shots of
bilongo—liquor fermented
from sugar and honey made by
Africans brought to Cuba where
slavers had them cutting cane
another act of transformation
the poor man's rum—balm for the ache
of laboring the *alisios*
brushing the skin a lover's hand.

NOTES

Our group of U.S. writers and ecocritics was hosted in Havana by the Antonio Nuñez Jimenez Foundation for Nature and Humanity, whose work fosters a Cuban society informed by environmental conscience. Since 1990 they have supported "people's plots," vacant state property set aside for people who want to grow food on urban ruins.

For an historical view of Professor Felipe Poey y Aloy (1799–1891), I've relied upon "Sketch of Felipe Poey" by David Jordan, *Popular Science Monthly*, August 1884.

I am indebted to Robert Duncan's poem "Often I Am Permitted to Return to a Meadow."

Chapter Eleven

Weight

Sylvia Torti

> I believe in the divinity of my essence; I feel and watch and believe in the wretchedness of my existence. And yet I seem, involuntarily, to acquiesce in my own wretchedness. What am I?
>
> —José Martí, from his notebook, circa 1872–1873

Like most Americans, I have a weight problem. According to "mi pareja," I've been on a diet since the day he met me, losing and gaining the same seven pounds over and over. Of course, he's right. I lack discipline. I like imported cheese, bread, and cured meats, chips, salsa, guacamole. The list goes on. One day, I overhear my son telling a friend that when his mother announces she's going on a diet, the first thing she asks him to do is to bring home some Doritos and M&Ms. Apparently, my habits are cyclical and predictable and highly counterproductive.

My father has escaped the dull Pampa winter of Argentina and is visiting me in Utah. We have one major point of difference. I hate to run errands. He loves to run errands, so I wait for his visits and we go together to drop off donations and shop for food, clothes, nuts, and bolts. There are so many things to buy, so many needs to keep the house in order, so many recipes to try. We make and scratch off lists, collect and discard receipts, and forget things so often that every project requires repeat trips to the store.

While in the car, we talk. These conversations are precious to me. Some of the stories I've heard before, like when a fellow student, "The Sicilian Beast," wanted to beat him up in seventh grade. Some are new. Recently he told me that as medical students, they had to create their own study materials. He and his friends climbed down into the public cemetery and spent hours sorting through piles of skeletons. They boiled the bones in a cauldron, some still with human material attached, and then painted them with a kind of shellac. "I slept with those bones in a box under my bed for six years," he tells me, "and when I finished medical school, I gave them to my cousin who was just starting."

"Well, at least those people were recycled and reused," I say.

"Whether they liked it or not," he says.

Today, I tell him about my recent trip to Havana. I grew up with a lot of talk about Cuba. Over dinner my father told my sisters and me about the revolution that toppled Batista, the U.S.A.-supported, repressive dictator. My mother railed against the complicity of religion in Latin American governments. Before I could even understand Spanish, my father taught me to recite poems by the great revolutionary, José Martí. These were stories of a society built on education and healthcare, a culture steeped in literary traditions, where the importance of words and speeches and literature were central to the expression of what it meant to be human. Later, in my twenties, after my mother's covert trip to the island, we learned that the country was not the utopia we'd hoped for. Her visit coincided with the "Special Period" of the 1990s after the island had lost critical economic support from the Soviet Union. There was widespread repression of people who didn't conform (e.g., gays), political detentions, and extensive control of the media. People were poor, and most disturbingly, they were hungry.

For the next twenty-five years, Cuba fell off my radar.

I was invited to Havana to participate in a meeting of American and Cuban writers interested in place, literature, and the environment. We were welcomed by Armando, who had organized the meeting, and quickly ferried into town, windows open. The humid afternoon air was a nice respite from Salt Lake's winter. As we passed the enormous José Martí statue, I recited "Cultiva una Rosa Blanca," which begins like this:

Cultivo una rosa blanca
en junio como enero
para el amigo sincero

I cultivate a white rose
in June as in January
for the sincere friend
(Torti translation)

It's a poem I likely would have forgotten except that a few years ago I rememorized it so that I could teach my son to recite it for his grandfather's eightieth birthday. Now, having memorized it both as a child and adult, carried it through the years, a momentous birthday, and now Cuba, it's become part of me. Something I cannot forget.

For days, we enjoyed Havana: the intersection of the colonial alongside the Caribbean, flowers with butterflies, torrents of rain, and easy-going people. The mantra: reuse, repair, and recycle was very much apparent—everything from the 1950s cars, to the practical bike taxis, and the leaf-woven pots at a garden that grows native plants for revegetation. As we walked through the butterfly garden, talking about the changes soon to be coming to Cuba with the opening of exchange with the United States, Armando said, "We want the internet. We don't want McDonalds."

Our meetings took place at the Antonio Jimenez Foundation for Humans and Nature. Jimenez (1923–1998) was a geographer, naturalist, and explorer who participated in the Revolution with Fidel. He served as the Cuban ambassador to Peru, was an avid advocate of cultural and biological diversity, and in 1987 he organized and directed an epic, traditional canoe expedition down the Amazon traveling ten thousand miles and passing through twenty countries with participants from each nation and culture.

The vision of the Foundation is of a Cuban society with a well-developed environmental conscience that recognizes nature as part of its identity. The house, museum, and libraries are filled with cabinets of curiosities, papers and books written by Jimenez, and an extensive collection of original portraits of prominent Latin American writers and activists. Our readings and discussions took place in his library. Fidel had just passed away. There were photographs of him everywhere, and you could feel the weight of a communal mourning.

The trip was replete with moments of insight and novel perspectives on Cuba, literature, and environmental work; but most poignant for me was the moment when Armando, on the last day in his summary statement, said, "We thank the Americans for the embargo because it saved us from the perversion of commodities."

I've been thinking about those words ever since. The perversion of commodities.

My father and I are at REI and I'm trying to find a hat. Soon I'll be going to Montana to teach an integrated minor called Ecology and Legacy, which puts ecology at the foundation and builds biology, humanities, and critical land art courses from that base. At seven thousand feet and open sky, the sun is unrelenting, and somehow in the past year, I've lost my broad brimmed hat. At the store, I'm going through the various styles, trying to find one that will cover my face and neck and not fly off my head. My father does what he does in every store. He shakes his head, walks around, and takes pictures. "So much stuff," he says. He texts these pictures to family and friends in Argentina.

I try on hats. They're all too big. Apparently, I have a smaller-than-average head. At some point, it occurs to me to move over to the children's section where I find a child's hat that fits me just fine, and it's only $28.00 instead of $78.00. I look around the youth section. Everywhere I look, I see big children. Milk and cereal-fed beefy faces. I start thinking. I need some pants. Maybe? Indeed, as I move through the rack, I see a few smalls, some mediums, larges, extra-larges, and extra-extra larges. I take the extra-large and the extra-extra-large and race to try them on, delighted by the fact that these pants are a fraction of the cost. I step into the extra-large size first and as I pull them up over my hips, I realize that not only do they fit, but they're slightly loose. Maybe all my hiking and running is working. I turn side to side as I look in the mirror, feeling a certain smugness. I am *not* an extra-extra-large kid! But then I stop and think, since when did children come in extra-extra-large?

I come out of the stall and see my dad over by the camping gear. I watch him pick up a specialized coffee maker and then another and another. When he comes over to the hat section, he echoes Armando. "Who needs all of this stuff?"

The next day we're at Costco. Salt Lake City has the biggest Costco in the world, I tell him. He is drawn to a freezer with whole hanging lambs, boxed pigs, and frozen ducks. He raises his eyebrows and snaps his phone camera again and again. Aisles and aisles of food, plastic plates, milk products, batteries, clothes, books. In my dieting, I've become obsessed with fatness. Everywhere I look, there are fat parents and fat children. We're all fat. We're pushing huge carts of food in bulk quantities down enormous aisles piled ground to ceiling with stuff. Mostly food stuff. All along the aisles while we walk, there are servers passing out food. We eat. We buy. We eat and we buy.

REI and Costco have a good bit in common, I realize. Both are warehouses full of factory bulk products, which give you the sense that you're shopping smartly, saving money. Hell, they both even buck the trend and stay closed on Black Friday so that families might enjoy the holiday and get outdoors. Ironically, the bounty of Costco results in our need for extra-extra-large kids pants, creating an REI of products that violate the premise of its own ideal—the active lifestyle.

A day after Costco, I read a *JAMA* article on obesity. I learn: 35–37 percent of American adults are "obese" (a BMI over 30) and another 30–40 percent are overweight (a BMI between 25–30). That means only 29 percent of people are within a normal weight range. We're eating five hundred more calories today than we did in the 1970s. No wonder I can buy kid's clothes.

I do a little research on Cuba and find a paper, "Obesity reduction and its possible consequences: What can we learn from Cuba's Special Period?" That was the time when the USSR could no longer support Cuba and the country suffered from a severe lack of fuel and food. What did Cuba do? It imported 1.2 million Chinese bikes, produced another 500,000 internally, and gave them out. During the same time, without fertilizers and pesticides, people started an urban and local farming movement call organopónicos. The government brought in experts from Australia to teach permaculture, and then a cadre of small organic farmers were deployed across the country to teach others.

During this time, energy intake per capita gradually decreased and the proportion of physically active adults increased from 30 percent to 67 percent. These changes affected the whole population and resulted in widespread, modest weight loss (i.e., 5 percent–6 percent of body weight, incidentally, the exact amount I'm hoping to lose) as well as a decline in all-cause mortality and deaths from diabetes and cardiovascular disease.

I'm thinking about gluttony—a gluttony that's not uniquely American, but rather the rapaciousness of mechanized cultures unconscious of their fundamental environmental limits. It's worth remembering that the Cubans didn't make their ecological shifts willingly. They were forced. The issue is not national, but one that arises from the modern, global culture obsessed with growing. An economy tied to increases in GDP, Dow Jones growth, and wealth. An economy blind to mortality and natural limits.

Should we starve? Certainly not, though we gag on commodities like a goose being stuffed for *fois gras*. As we get fatter, we're losing our ecology, and what we lose ecologically, and by extension, spiritually, we're gaining in weight. This isn't just fat around the waist, but a psychological weight. A weight that inevitably becomes depression, heart attack, diabetes, and death.

"*Mi pareja*" tells me that I worry too much about my weight. Of course, he's right. Some of it is vanity, but I also see in my body the culture in which I live. While my extra weight is a personal stress, I experience our collective fattening as a sad, sad moment. There is a sense of shame. Our culture shames our individual bodies when in reality, it is the collective body that is a disgrace.

I'm thinking of how I might design a new kind of diet. A regimen that rejects the perversity of commodities in exchange for time spent consuming that which is fleeting and invisible. The immaterial, like a poem, that comes to reside in the marrow of our bones.

I desire days organized around the kind of ecological identity that Jimenez proposed. Days in which I accumulate only observations and memories. I desire an ecology that includes conversations, cabinets of curiosities, and the slow exercise of reading and telling. Time spent listening to my father's recollections of an Argentina that existed before, and his reflections on what those memories mean to him now. Not food or clothes or devices, I realize that what I most desire is the real and fulfilling sustenance of our individual and communal lives.

WORKS CONSULTED

Manuel, Franco, MD PhD, Pedro Orduñez, MD PhD, Benjamín Caballero, MD PhD, and Richard S. Cooper, MD. 2008. "Obesity reduction and its possible consequences: What can we learn from Cuba's Special Period?" *Canadian Medical Association Journal* 178 (8): 1032–34. April 8.

Yang, Lin, Graham A. Colditz. 2015. Prevalence of overweight and obesity in the United States, 2007–2012. *JAMA Intern Med* 175(8): 1412–23.

Chapter Twelve

The Cuba Poems

Robert Michael Pyle

INTRODUCTION

When I was invited by Professor David Taylor to come to Cuba with the other writers, I was both excited and intimidated. Of course I knew it would be fun: I would be traveling with both old friends and new acquaintances, which is always exciting. But, though I have traveled quite a bit in Latin America, my Spanish is poor, I had almost no experience in the Caribbean, and my strengths lie far more in the natural history of the countryside than the culture of the city. I wondered what I might possibly bring to his exchange.

I had no such doubts, however, about what I would gain as a person, a traveler, and a writer. Fresh experience in wholly novel places always enriches, if one merely keeps an open mind and open eyes and other senses. And that's the way it was. Walking, listening, watching, smelling, I took my paltry language into the streets and parks by day and night and simply opened myself to the place, the people. I have seldom felt so warmly welcome anywhere, or so quickly immersed in new and stimulating sensations. I could have gone on and on, and that was just a few days, in a few parts of Havana. Think what a whole year, ranging out around the island, might reveal! But we had what we had, and I am very happy to have been a part of it.

These poems tell a little of what I found.

RMP
May 30, 2017
Gray's River, Washington

I. ABANDONED IN HAVANA

Nothing since that empanada at the airport
but a couple of beers. So when seven o'clock comes
and nobody shows up for dinner, I step out
to forage on my own. Cuba is new,
my Spanish sucks, and I am none too sure.
But somehow I find the porch of El Presidente,
a Carib fish filet, an Argentinian Carmeniere,
as the old Dodges and DeSotos rumble past
and the pretty women blow by on the cool breeze
in the palms. A young man places a helmet
on his girlfriend's head, they mount a motorbike.
Kids gather on the sidewalk for the hotel's wi-fi.
Fidel was buried yesterday, so after nine days of silence
the music starts again tonight. Down the veranda
a four-woman band—singer in white, plus maracas,
congas, electric bass, and acoustic flute—blazes
through a tight Cubana set. A shot of Cuban rum
has landed in my hand. I guess I'll make it
through my abandonment, after all.

II. ON THE MALECON

After the day, after a nap, after rum at sunset, I walk
down to the Bay, the long seawall called the Malecon. Turn
south toward the river. Along the Malecon lovers caress,
runners sweat, yogis stretch. Fishermen cast out, some with poles,
some just spools. A boy shows me the sea-perch he's just pulled in.
Waves slap over coral to the seawall on my right, make
the sidewalk green and slick with algae. Fumes slap
from the other side, sea of traffic where schools of green
'54 Fords and blue '49 Chevys tool the broad four-lane.
Busking *guitarreros* and prostitutes troll for customers,
languid boys with cell phones, girls arm-in-arm in short shorts
and bright skirts. A plastic bag, blown up with sea breeze,
races me all along the Malecon to the Rio Almendares.

III. OFF THE MALECON

The dark neighborhoods are quiet but
for soft voices of children in the streets.
Doors open, bare-chested men before TVs,
women talking like soft birds in the night.
In a little corner bakery I buy a sticky bun
for a peso. A black woman buying bread says
"You should stay here in Havana!" and

the white baker nods his agreement. "Here,"
she says, "there is no color."

IV. THE CATS OF HAVANA

are black and white. Okay, a few gingers and tabbies,
a calico or two. But on the whole, black and white. Also
many are polydactyl, like Hemingway's cats in Key West.

It is said the cats of Cuba disappeared into cooking pots
after the collapse of the Soviet Union, when hunger hit
the country hard. But now they're back. It is said

that all sorts of changes are coming, now that the U.S.A.
is back too. Will *yanqui* dollars improve lives here?
Or just make the rich richer? Will this invasion work,
where the Bay of Pigs failed? Everyone wonders
what's to come.

Meanwhile, the cats of Havana carry on
their nightly prowl.

V. THE BATS OF HAVANA

Whisk past my shoulder
leaving echoes
of ink and gauze.

VI. THE TOUR

David takes me on a long and arduous walk
through the streets of Central to the Old Town.
On the way, the university. A young man approaches,
tells us he is Ivan, a student. Leads us on a tour
through backstreets. "Here is Fidel's house as a student!"
"Here is the bar where Fidel and Che plotted and drank—
at that very table!" "We should drink here too!" So we do—
to the *Revolucionarias*, to us, to *Cuba y USA*—on us.
Afterward David tells me that Ivan was no student,
and we were taken for a ride. Those shrines? Who knows.
No matter. I've been taken for worse of a fool
before. It was cheap, an experience, a story to tell;
and Ivan ate well that night. Later, our friends recount
meeting two professors at the university,
who took them on a tour. . . .

VII. SITTING IN THE STUDY CARREL

in Antonio Núñez Jiménez Foundation for Man and Nature.
Núñez Jiménez , the great geographer, fought with Che,
had Fidel's lifelong friendship. These eight carrels came
from Castro's old college. Pink silk upholstered chairs,
glass-topped, brass-lit, slanted mahogany writing desks.
Theses, manuscripts, and books fill tall shelves all 'round.
Soft murmurs of scholars and poets through sliding doors.
How I would love to write more than these few lines here.
Oh! WHAT I would write here!

VIII. AMONG THE WRITERS

Cuban and American writers sit down together
in two facing rows of square tables, each a display
case of fossils, formations, minerals, medals,
regalia, and souvenirs of *La Revolución*. Tall shelves
hold Núñez Jiménez's manuscripts on one side,
his bound books of photographs on the other.
Che, Fidel, and their comrades-in-arms peer
from framed black-and-white pictures on both walls.
We take turns reading our poems and papers up front.
Armando MCs, comments on each one, the way they do
here. The poems go mostly in their own language,
taken for their rhythm and flow. Luis translates lucidly, but
a long paper on gender in Cuban fairy tales is a challenge.
To be honest, we all find it a challenge, in either language.
But then, from between all the lines of arid scholarship,
comes this:
"I used to live in a pumpkin, inside a pumpkin patch."
And this:
"Make your baskets,
fill them up with butterflies and fireflies,
wait for me, and we will make a good party."
And, frankly? I would have come to Cuba just to hear that.

IX. AT THE WRITERS' UNION

(*La Unión de Escritores y Artistas de Cuba*)

We *yanqui* poets and scholars are invited
to a reception for a famous photographer,
a rare honor for outsiders. Our gifts of books
for the library are received without fanfare.

After the honoree speaks, wine is served. Look

around for someone I can speak with, pounce
on the owner of the only voice I savvy.
Leonardo, professor of English, is here
with his niece Yurisan and nephew Evelio.
Leonardo strongly resembles Barack Obama.
"Did you suffer any cases of mistaken identity," I ask,
"during the president's recent visit to Cuba?" "Only
once," he says. "It was the Belgian Ambassador."

X. IN THE BOTANIC GARDEN (*QUINTA DE LOS MOLINOS*)

On the bus to *La Quinta de los Molinos*, Luis talks
about the Rolling Stones. Their free concert
in Havana, he says, was the highlight of his life
so far. I tell him about Seattle in '94 and '05.
But now we are here. Marisela and Danielle guide
us through the Eco-Park, show us Bahaman swallowtails,
monarchs, and zebras in the *Mariposario*. Outside,
rusty bumblebees visit lilies, scarlet dragonflies skim
the koi pond, red-legged thrushes work the greenery.

When the rest leave for a hot walk through Havana Vieja,
I stay behind where gulf fritillaries and Baracoa skippers
haunt weedy corners. Later, forage smoky streets for lunch,
smuggle two baby bananas and a beer back into the garden.
On a bench beneath a bower, a nest above my head, cooled
by a breeze off the dragonfly pond, two more hours to explore
this oasis in the teeming city before I catch an old car back—
in this place of notorious poverty, why do I feel so rich?

Chapter Thirteen

Restauración

Laura Ruíz Montes

Se reparan equipos electrodomésticos
zapatos y sillones
en cada esquina de la calle principal.
Se ofrecen cuchillas de afeitar
para depilar rostros
sacar puntas a los lápices
y recordar cuando con otros nombres
se acumulaban en todos los establecimientos.
Para recordar cuando padres y abuelos
salían del baño con la mejilla cortada
ponían la otra, a la tarde siguiente,
y volvían a salir, optimistas,
heridos y sangrantes.

Alguien pasa arreglando colchones y cocinas de gas.
Se desbloquean celulares,
se ponen pilas nuevas a relojes viejos.

Todo remite a objetos deteriorados y enfermos,
a una época anterior
donde las pertenencias estaban sanas
y creíamos iban a ser eternas.
Una época anterior
donde padres y abuelos

al caer la noche
estiraban las piernas
para que subiéramos por el puente
y acariciáramos aquellas mejillas
lisas

olorosas
y pulcras
como si antes allí
no hubiera pasado nada.

RESTORATION

Laura Ruíz Montes
Translated by Margaret Randall

They repair household appliances,
shoes and armchairs,
on Main Street's every corner.
They offer razor blades
to shave faces
or sharpen pencils
reminding us of those other names
under which they once existed.
Reminding us when fathers and grandfathers
emerged from the bathroom with a cut on the cheek
and turned the other one, and the next afternoon
emerged again, optimistic,
wounded and bleeding.

Someone passes, fixing mattresses and gas stoves.
They unblock cell phones,
put new batteries in old watches.

Anything reminiscent of broken down things,
sick things from a previous era
when our belongings were healthy
and we thought they would last forever.

A previous era where each night
fathers and grandfathers
stretched out their legs
so we could climb the bridge
and caress those smooth cheeks,
fragrant and fresh
as if nothing had ever happened there before.

Chapter Fourteen

Lessons from Cuba

Blas Falconer

In December 2016, I traveled to Havana with several other Americans, artists and scholars, for a United States-Cuba writers' symposium. It was a time of great division and uncertainty both home and abroad. Only a month before we were to depart, Donald Trump, against all odds, was elected president of the United States, and days before we boarded our flight, Fidel Castro died.

As the plane approached the Cuban coastline, I pressed my forehead against the window. How many times had I done the same thing, approaching Puerto Rico's familiar shore, where my mother was born and raised, where I spent so many summers with my grandmother, my aunts, uncles, and cousins.

Arriving in Cuba, I couldn't help but compare the two places, the humid air, the landscape, the light, but also, the same rhythm of the language as our driver spoke, the same hustle in the street, that saunter, even the same faces that, in my forty-five years, I've come to recognize as family.

But this wasn't Puerto Rico, of course, having its own unique identity, its own history, its own particular struggles. At the University of Havana, a professor showed us around the campus, along the streets of Old Havana, explaining the significance of historical landmarks. Stepping into a small shop, he pointed to the cartons of eggs, the bags of flour, describing how the food vouchers worked.

"And yet, we must find other ways to supplement our income," he said. "Even professors."

As we sat over a drink, he explained how their economy collapsed with the Soviet Union, how proud he still was of their health care system, describing Cuban physicians as the best in the world, how Cuba was the first to send help whenever there was a medical crisis.

"HIV/AIDS, Zika, the West African Ebola Epidemic. We go where no one else dares to."

"What will happen, now," we asked. "Now that Fidel is gone?"

He looked at us gravely, "Who knows? "We accept change, we welcome Americans, but we don't want to become the United States either. We don't want to lose ourselves."

How many times had I heard my grandmother voice similar concerns for Puerto Rico?

At the symposium, I spoke of Puerto Rican poetry and its use of metaphors drawn from the island's tropical landscape to promote the Independence movement, one that my grandmother enthusiastically supported. Others spoke on a range of different subjects, but many scholars addressed the environment, global warming, ecocriticism, the importance of preservation and education. Our coming together brought us great hope, eager as we were to hear each other out, to learn from one another.

It's been six months since our trip. If there was division at home before the U.S. election, it seems even more profound now.

"The United States of America, as we know it, is over," Joseph, my husband, said recently, and I couldn't help but think of our professor in Havana when we asked about Cuba's future. I couldn't help but think of my grandmother and Puerto Rico. Maybe Joseph's right.

I recently received a copy of *La Gaceta*, the Cuban literary journal, founded by Nicolás Guillén (1902–1989), the latest issue, in which my own essay from the symposium appears. It was sent to me by the current editor, Norberto Codina—also, a poet.

Among literary and critical pieces, I came across Laura Ruiz's poem, "Restauración" which begins by noting the many repair shops on the main street of town—Havana, I'm guessing—how there is a place to restore whatever has been broken.

The importance of restoring what has been broken seems particularly true to life in Cuba, with its decades of relative isolation, and a concept almost completely foreign in America, where everything seems disposable, where it often costs more to repair something than to buy new.

Toward the end of the poem, Ruiz turns to address how it is important to remember people long gone, whose bodies could no longer be unbroken or restored to their younger selves.

It is more than a nostalgic gesture for those who have died, but a celebration of their resilient spirit, and all the days that they did survive, thrived. In this time of uncertainty and despair and hopelessness, let Ruiz's dead be models to us all, models of the human spirit's will to fight, to continue, so that we might restore ourselves and restore one another—as individuals, as communities, as countries—time and again, for as long as we can.

In solidarity with Laura Ruiz and the sentiment of her poem, I offer my own, written for my grandmother, gone now, too, whose spirit and will I honor.

REVOLUTION

After Myrna Baez's "Platanal," Oil on Canvas

Plantain trees gather at the edge
of the orchard, clamor for light

in the foreground. They seem to grow
as one, as if they'd fill the field

and the mountains behind them,
leaves large and frayed. We stood

there, once, or someplace like it, so
here we are again, it seems,

years later, branches leaning over
the road, you in your long skirt,

looking out as if to recall something
you meant to do. *My country*, I hear

you say still. But if that's dusk
in the hills, you know what's

coming to the field. You'll stand
among them till there's nothing left

to see. I'll wait beside you, though
I don't know what we're waiting for.[1]

NOTE

1. When considering Myrna Baez's painting "Platanal," E. Carmen Ramos explains, "When Puerto Rico was a Spanish colony, artists like Francisco Oller depicted the plantain as both a key accoutrement to the *jibaro* (rural peasant) and a metaphor for the island's independent cultural identity."

Chapter Fifteen

El Trompo

In the Sierra Maestra with Guerrilla de Teatreros

David Taylor

Pedro Deymo Tasèt Viamonte handed me the top (*el trompo*) he had made from the fruit of a calabash or guira tree, hand-carved cedar, and a plastic bottle cap nailed in the top to hold it all together. In front of the children and adults who had walked for kilometers to be there, under the *chabola* (covered area) of palm fronds and thin logs, Pedro said:

> *Por favor, toma este trompo. Yo soy la última persona aquí que fabrica trompos para los niños. Cuéntale la historia a las personas en los Estados Unidos, diles que aquí aún hay alguien que los hace de la misma manera que mi padre y mis abuelos lo hicieron. Diles que es importante que todavía alguien sepa hacer estos trompos.*
>
> Please, take this top. I am the last person here that makes tops for the children. Tell this story to the people of the United States, tell them that here someone makes them in the same way my father and my grandfathers made them. Tell them that it is important that someone still makes these tops.

He handed me the trompo as though he was handing me his home, his history, his world.

I've had the good fortune of traveling to Cuba for a few years, back when there weren't as many Americans. My Cuban-American family helped me build relationships with professors at the University of Havana, and a new friend Ana Lopez at Tulane University helped me connect with writers such as Armando Fernandez and Norberto Codina. Another family member made way for me to meet Gisela Gonzales, president of Artes Escencias, Cuba's national performing arts organization. The initial goal was to create a study abroad class from the University of North Texas focused on sustainability in Cuba, but soon the conversations turned to collaborations, possible work, writing, and research. It's an obvious thing to say, but creating collaborations and follow-through between Cubans and Americans takes time, patience, and a slowly earned trust. Ours is a very complicated history.

Throughout these years, though, my Cuban colleagues and now dear friends have encouraged my work here, even though my Spanish is mediocre and my lily-white christian Texas background offers me little in cultural context. Thus, while they and I sometimes have a lot to overcome, I have always known that their encouragement and trust comes from a common concern: this precious, wobbling, blue *earth* we share, which now seems all too close to spinning off balance.

President Gisela Gonzales, in particular, wanted me to spend time with some of the theater groups who incorporate environmental awareness and outreach as part of their performances. One group, TECMA, often scours the landfill outside of Pinar del Rio to find usable materials to construct their costumes. They also teach a group of at-risk teenagers how to perform and walk on the *zancos* or stilts as part of their training to become licensed actors in a group. Other groups, such as Teatro de los Elementos, have even taken up sustainable farming and restoring native forests as part of their artistic mission. Teatro de la Forteleza and Director Atilio Caballero have put together performances to raise awareness of water shortages in Juragua. Teatro Tuyo's performance *Gris* keenly points to what is being lost through environmental degradation through pantomime. Last, Guerilla de Teatreros, a group in Bayamo, for over twenty-five years, has taken up a yearly, month-long pilgrimage across the remote Sierra Maestra to visit the small *communidades* with the goal of bringing art and entertainment to *camposinos*. They carry with them their personal belongings and bedding, as well as costumes, musical instruments, and anything they might need for a performance, often five to ten kilometers a day. Gisela said, "You need to see the work these groups are doing. You need to show Americans what these artists are doing—how committed they are to their communities, to their place, to your and my environment. You need to tell their stories."

My previous research trips in 2014 and 2015 to Cuba did little to prepare me for the fifteen-hour overnight bus ride from Havana to Bayamo in the eastern Sierra Maestra. Viazul buses are mostly filled by Cubans traveling to visit family or for work, but there are usually a couple of young tourists making their way across the length of the island. The bus stops every forty-five minutes to an hour at one of the larger cities, and takes on more passengers the closer it gets to either Havana or Santiago. I was worried I'd miss my stop in Bayamo, so I did not sleep, listening intently as the bus driver softly announced the city only once before stopping. I arrived in Bayamo at 5 a.m., my backpack and I ready for some sleep.

Rene Reyes, founder and director of Guerilla de Teatreros, met me at the bus station and took me to my hotel downtown. I fell asleep to the sounds of people sweeping the flower petals of the sidewalk by the park across the street. A soft rain fell offering me a lullaby.

Cuba represents a wonderful case study for the possibility of using the arts, media, and cultural traditions as a means of encouraging citizens to adopt environmentally sustainable practices. Since the 1990s, Cuba has been in the unique situation of being forced to address sustainable agricultural and environmental practices. Surprisingly, few societies currently match the educational and legislative commitments and actions toward environmental and food sustainability that Cuba offers. Because of its innovations, Cuba is the only country that has reached "sustainable development" status as designated by the World Wildlife Federation. According to the World Wildlife Fund (WWF) report in 2006 Cuba was the only country in the world to reach this impressive sustainability standing, because the country covers their present needs without compromising the ability of future generations to meet their own needs. Cuba demonstrates and makes it possible to imagine future radical possibilities that can be used to analyze and challenge the unsustainable paradigm that presently dominates the world (WWF). Cuba is a complex, complicated "real world" socialist country that since the 1990s has had a fundamentally different relationship with the environment than capitalist and past "socialist" countries. The WWF honor indicates success reaching the United Nations human development index and minimal per-person "ecological footprint." Over a period of about twenty years during the "Special Period" after the collapse of the Soviet Union and its subsidies to Cuba, this island nation transitioned from an industrial-agricultural system of large farms treated with fossil-fuel-based pesticides, insecticides, and fertilizers to smaller, local, and organic farms and urban gardens. Much of this change was out of necessity, as Cuba could no longer rely on Soviet agricultural methods. As governments and advocacy groups around the world have found, laws, policies, and incentives may do a lot to encourage changes in daily choices toward sustainability, but in Cuba, this long-term change has additionally involved social tendencies and traditions and actively engaged the arts to make environmental awareness and sustainability a part of culture.

The place of arts in Cuban culture is immediate—music, literature, visual and performing arts are vital part of the average citizen's daily life. Readings, exhibits, and performances of all types are generally well attended and inexpensive for citizens. It is well-understood by sociologists that community outreach in the performing arts—whether it be in the form of dance, theater, music, or other public performances—strengthens cultural experiences and buy-in in terms of shared knowledge and experiences. Public performing arts have a critically important place in Cuban culture. What makes them extraordinarily effective was that they used national heritages, folklore, traditional and mass culture, and the combining of the literal and the metaphorical to make statements about the importance of social justice and caring for the environment.

Rene sees the Guerilla de Teatreros' work as his part in the revolution—to bring arts and education to the people in rural villages in the mountains, who might otherwise have no access. He had arranged a three-day trip for the group and I into a more accessible part of the mountains, not far from Bayamo. He wanted to give me a glimpse into the work they do, without having to commit to a month-long stay. Organizing twenty theater performers and their belongings is no small task, so it took one open bed truck and a "guarandinga"—a dump truck modified to be a bus—to get all of us and our things to "Communidad Victorino," a town of two hundred people. The group is made up of Rene, Yamis, his daughter, and a few folks who've been a part of the group for a decade or so, but mostly young folks in their twenties who can play, sing, and dance as well as perform acrobatics, magic shows, and comedy skits. The ride from Bayamo to Victorino is bumpy, but the young folks sing and pass around the guitar, switching songs between Bob Marley, reggaeton, and traditional son. I offer them in return a few old Texas folk standards, such as "Fruelein" and "Red River Valley." They laugh out loud about the twang and drawl in my singing. I tell them I am a *guajiro* (country guy) so it's OK to sound that way.

Our housing is the former patient rooms in a generally closed hospital that serves a wide swath of the northern slope of the Sierra. We unload our foam pads and clothes bags. Rene shows me the restroom/outhouse, promising me good Cuban coffee soon. Our cook is a local who knows how to make a dinner of rice, pork, and beans for a large group with two large pots and an open flame. The hospital is to be our starting point for two trips to perform—one to El Queso, a village of fifty people or so about four kilometers away, and the latter to Las Canarias, a place even smaller about five kilometers away in the opposite direction. The people who live in the area know when Guerilla de Teatreros is in town; word travels fast for a place where cell phones are useless and landlines are not common. By now, some of the adults and parents were children the first time they met Rene, Yamis, and the group; they make sure to bring their children to see the performances.

Our first trip to El Queso is a short trip, but the river crossings demand that we lift the musical instruments high above our heads to keep them dry. The performance is held in a small schoolhouse. The actors begin with acrobatics as well as comedy skits, singing well-known songs, and dancing. We are served coffee, grown in the village, but we also help in grinding the coffee in the mortar and pestle. On our return trip, an old man who lived near the trail had heard the group is in the area and asks if they can come to his house. He is too weak to get outside, but he wants to hear music. The musicians happily go to his house and play a few traditional songs, "El Carratero" and "Dos Gardenias" among others. He smiles and tries to sing a bit of a song from his youth. "Thank you," he says. "Thank you."

Our trip the next day to Las Canarias has no rivers to cross but is a difficult uphill climb. Again, the actors carry everything with them, stopping now and then to rest. By the time we arrive in Las Canarias, the *camposinos* have set up a table of coffee, fresas, maize, choyote, bananas, and mango. After a brief ceremonious greeting, the actors and I are allowed to eat all we want and to carry the rest back with us. It is their thanks to Guerilla de Teatreros for coming here to perform.

At this time is when Pedro came forward to present me with the *trompo*. I was at first embarrassed, standing next to him at the center of attention. I am not Cuban; I am the observer here not the focal point. Then, why I wondered, why had he walked so far to hand me this object so that he could tell me to tell this story. The group gave their performance and delighted all, promising to come back within the next year.

In the seven months since Pedro gave me the trompo and asked me to tell his story, I have had more than a few sleepless nights wondering what he meant, *Diles que es importante que todavía alguien sepa hacer estos trompos*. I keep it on my desk to make sure it is part of my daily writing and work. The story I am supposed to be telling is only partly coming to me, but each day it emerges a bit clearer.

The word *trompo* primarily refers to a *juegete,* a child's toy like the one Pedro handed to me. But it can also mean to spin, like a car out of control, or a clumsy person tripping over most everything, perhaps a poor dancer with no rhythm, and maybe even a drunken person staggering along the street. Sometimes, we think our worlds are separate, the United States or Cuba, New York or Bayamo, Las Canarias or any small village in Montana. But we are bound together, riding this great *trompo* spinning, wobbling, possibly falling out of control. Rising sea levels and higher full moon tides threaten our coastal cities, saltwater intrusion changing the ecology of our marshes and estuaries, weather patterns becoming more extreme between drought and devastating hurricanes: we share these. Thus we recognize that we are both on this *trompo*, and that we share that story. We need to tell that story over and over in every language and culture, and remind others to remember and tell it too; otherwise, no one will know how to make *trompos*; no one will remember how to act in shared responsibility.

I must tell his story, but it is also the story of the Cuban people I have met and the friends who have helped me, my parents' story, your parents' stories,

Cuban stories, American stories, all of our stories. Perhaps in sharing our stories and our awareness of the need to care for our places and our planet, we begin to see we share so much. Maybe then, we will have the courage to work together to pass on the caring and action and live with a bit more wisdom.

Chapter Sixteen

Something Wonderful and Surreal

American Ecocritics and Environmental Writers Contemplate Exile in Cuba as Donald Trump Eyes the White House

Scott Slovic

There was something wonderful and surreal about the first formal meeting of Cuban and American ecocritics and environmental writers during our gathering in Havana in December 2016. The American contingent gathered in Miami for the short hop to Havana, with poetic lepidopterist Robert Michael Pyle arriving at the meeting point after a red-eye from the West Coast, brightly clad in an Aloha shirt and expedition gear, looking like a cross between a Kona-bound snowbird and Alexander von Humboldt. Flying in from New York, Atlanta, Tucson, Salt Lake City, Los Angeles, northern Idaho, and southwestern Washington, we reveled in our own sense of community as environmental writers and in the sheer strangeness of our departure for Cuba, a place most of us had only dreamed about, perhaps never even imagining that we would set foot there, so long had Cuba been a nearby but forbidden land for most Americans. Of course we were not the first group of American writers to seek refuge and adventure in Cuba—Hemingway had famously done so before the revolution, and as recently as 2004 David Gessner has pursued his passion for osprey by following the autumn migration to Cuba while at work on the manuscript that would become *Soaring with Fidel: An Osprey Odyssey from Cape Cod to Cuba and Beyond* (2007).

Our squad's objectives were less focused than Gessner's interest in osprey, but food, drink, and escapism were certainly in the mix. Our Cuban sensory experience began at Café Versailles in Miami International Airport by way of empanadas, guava and cheese pastelitos, and Cuban coffee, known as *cortados*. For the American academics, the Monday morning departure for a Caribbean island in early December felt like playing hooky, ducking out from the fall term just before finals week. Those of us coming from the Rocky Mountain region of northern Idaho and Utah, in particular, felt a certain glee to be heading south just at the onset of an unusually bitter winter—this excursion represented a final gust of warm air before months and months of ice and snow. But one thing we all felt in common, as we drank our cortados and collected our thoughts for the upcoming environmental symposium in Havana, was a sense of deep and bewildered dread in the immediate wake of the November 2016 American presidential election. We had a sense that something very bad had happened, but none of us at that point understood just how ominous Donald Trump's election was—the rogues gallery of racists and plutocrats and nature haters had not yet been appointed as Trump's cabinet, but the writing was on the wall.

As we assembled at the gate to await our half-hour flight across the sea, I began to lose track of the purpose of our visit. Most of the people waiting to board the American Airlines flight seemed to be white American tourists, heading toward warmer climes in early December, excited by the prospect of a direct flight to an island that had been off limits to American tourists until a few months earlier. This entourage of writers and scholars was heading to an academic event of some kind, but only one of us, David Taylor, had met our Cuban counterparts before and had a clear idea of the program for our visit. The trip to Cuba felt as if we were stepping off a cliff or perhaps diving into a deep sea, heading toward an unknown reality.

I had been thinking quite a bit about unknown realities and dreaded possibilities in the weeks prior to our departure for Havana on December 5, almost exactly a month after the American presidential election had shocked the world, sending Donald Trump, an avowed misogynist, immigrant-hater, and antienvironmentalist, on his way to become the 45th president of the United States. At the time, we had no idea how monstrous and incompetent Trump would be in his presidential role, but even the threat of his presidency sent shudders through our group of progressive scholars and writers. It had been my intention to travel to Cuba and tell the story of the "roots and branches" of the Association for the Study of Literature and Environment during my brief talk at the Encuentro Literatura y Medio Ambiente, but even as we waited to board our flight in Miami I began to have misgivings about what I should say, what I could offer, to my Cuban colleagues and my American friends. My entire narrative about the advanced state of ecocriticism and environmental humanities research in the United States and throughout the world had begun to crack apart in light of the political unheaval and dark future for environmental protection promised by the newly elected thugs in our country. Rather than planning to reach out a helping hand to Cuban environmentalists and guide them toward the international community of environmental thinkers, I found myself hoping we might ourselves be thrown a lifeline by the Cubans, who had experienced half a century of isolation from much of the world community, certainly from the United States, and seemed none the worse for the experience.

The actual flight from Florida to Cuba involved taking off over aquamarine water followed almost immediately by preparations to land. As we dropped lower and lower over a green island, I was struck by the complete absence of traffic on red dirt roads not far from the capital city of Havana, just the opposite of the crowded highways of Miami. I'm a great lover of empty roads, often seeking out the most isolated highways in the American West—such as Highway 50 across the interior of Nevada or the Pasco-Kahlotus Highway through the southeastern corner of Washington State—for my driving routes back home. The empty roads near Havana gave me the feeling that Cuba might be a good place, a familiar and somehow stable environment, at a time when everything back in the United States was going haywire.

Of course, upon landing in Havana, the reality of automobiles and urban noises set in. But Cuba appeared to be a place of warm colors and smiling people. Buildings were painted pastel pink, orange, and blue, and brightly colored antique automobiles filled the roads from the airport to the capital, just as advertised in a thousand tourist guides. Hotels and cafés served cuba libres and mojitos and offered lavish servings of fish, beans, and rice on placemats made of vinyl records. Even the ratty buildings of Havana Vieja, exposing bent rebar and bony residents with nothing to do but sit in doorways and gape at the parade of humanity on the street, were a welcome escape from the thought of handing the American nuclear codes and the keys to the Environmental Protection Agency over to corporate thieves and scientific illiterates. The lack of snow on clean but crumbling sidewalks was a relief, too, after weeks of slippery, freezing weather in northern Idaho. But after only a few hours of ambling along the quiet streets near El Presidente Hotel and the Malecón ring road next to the seawall north of Havana, it became clear that Cuba is not a paradise, but a real place, fraught with exhaust fumes and poverty. The lovely colonial villas that now house government ministries were once family homes until confiscated by the revolutionary regime in the 1950s—and the former owners of these properties, living in exile over in the United States, will never acquiesce to the loss of family wealth in the name of socialism. The placidity of Cuba, as we experienced it during our brief time in Havana, was as illusory as the stability of American society had been during the Obama administration that preceded Trump's ascendance.

The Miramar neighborhood of western Havana boasts elegant colonial buildings and mature gardens full of bougainvillea and tropical plants. We arrived at the Fundación Antonio Nuñez Jiménez on the morning of the third day of our visit to Cuba, having been handed a brief program for our symposium upon arrival in the country. There would be nine brief readings and academic talks, intermixed with consecutive translation into Spanish or English, followed by a visit to the Jardín Botánico y Mariposario.

Our presentations, to a great extent, offered gestures of bridge-building to our new friends from across the Caribbean. Robert Michael Pyle, imagining the famous old cars on the Cuban roads, read a poem about his beloved "Powdermilk," the vehicle that had transported him thousands of miles through the American countryside in pursuit of butterflies. He and Alison Hawthorne Deming, who read later that morning, spoke of monarch butterflies, the "blizzard of orange," as Alison put it, that is one of nature's most cherished spectacles and yet is endangered through the carelessness of human action, our use of chemical pesticides and our devastation of forest habitat. Mayra Beatriz Martinez analyzed the stereotypical representations of women in the writings of José Martí, one of the giant figures in Cuban letters, calling for an appreciation of "natural women," an acceptance of women as they truly are. American writer and biologist Sylvia Torti, in an essay about her work as a biologist in Chiapas, Mexico, demonstrated the complexity and reality of human consciousness of nature, balancing subjective and objective ways of knowing the world. Armando Fernandez invoked the necessities of reusing and retaining durable goods, such as old cars, and the imperatives of migration in the Americas, such as butterflies traveling southward and Latin American workers going north. Itinerant English-French-American ecocritic Wendy Harding spoke of having migrated again and again to many places as a student and visiting professor and her desire to plant roots somewhere in the world. Puerto Rican-American poet Blas Falconer echoed Wendy's ideas of rootlessness and made them poignant by recalling his relationships with family members back in Puerto Rico, evoking the nostalgia of exile. Mariana Serra García suggested in her discussion of Cuban author Excilia Saldaña that Nigerian immigrants, brought to Cuba as slaves centuries ago, have had a lasting and important influence in Cuban ideas about the nonhuman world—so transience and rootlessness actually do serve a purpose in how cultures evolve toward new ideas and new relationships with the world.

In addition to presentations emphasizing the coherence and stability of human and animal migrations, our December 2016 symposium had strong overtones of uncertainty and fear, of warning and confusion. David Taylor spoke of *el trompo*, the spinning top that is a popular children's toy in Latin America, suggesting that our wonderful Earth is but a wobbly blue top, less stable than it may appear. He urged listeners at the symposium, fellow writers, to "tell the story that has to be told." Armando Fernandez also struck a sober tone is his comments on various presentations, arguing that human society has not matured over time and that we must change our cultures if our species is to have a viable future. He called for democratic, transparent solutions to social and environmental problems, pointing out, as climate justice scholars and activists have often stated, that global climate change especially threatens small islands, such as Cuba, that do not themselves produce most of the greenhouse gases that are imperiling the planet. Havana was the only area in Cuba that most of the American speakers had seen, yet Armando pointed out that this was the least admirable part of Cuba, a "negative example" of an environmental society, because of all the waste produced by the urban population. The real positive changes that are developing in Cuba are occurring, he said, in the interior of the country, far from the capital.

I listened to the lectures and comments of the fifteen people who attended our intimate symposium and found myself wondering what we were doing in this elegant meeting room of natural objects encased in glass, words encased in books, and photos of Fidel Castro encircling the room (Fidel with his trusted advisors, Fidel giving speeches, Fidel playing golf), suggesting outreach to the broader realm of public life. "What are we doing here?" I asked at the beginning of my talk. "Overcoming loneliness? Amusing ourselves? Planting seeds? Building bridges?" The Environmental Humanities is a proliferating conglomeration of disciplines, rapidly expanding in many parts of the world. Over the years I had participated in dozens of similar gatherings in smoke-filled rooms in Tokyo's Shinjuku District, while walking through the statuesque ruins of the Mamallapuram World Heritage Site in southern India, and climbing the pyramids of Teotihuacan with scientists and writers in central Mexico, among many others. In the months prior to the Havana symposium, I had listened to similar lectures in a medieval convent in Perpignan, France, and a baroque castle that had been transformed into a university building in Wroclaw, Poland. The Havana symposium, though, reminded me especially of the late-night meeting of mainland Chinese and Taiwanese ecocritics at a tea house in Beijing, organized by Professor Lu Shuyuan, the elder statesman of Chinese ecocriticism, during a 2008 conference at Tsinghua University. In the informal setting of the tea house, cloaked by comforting darkness, scholars from societies that were at odds politically were able to befriend each other and form pacts of mutual encouragement. I felt something similar was happening in Miramar, Havana, as our small group shared ideas under the watchful eyes of Antonio Nuñez Jiménez and Fidel Castro, who were present in paintings and photos.

In my remarks to the group, in addition to offering my personal post-election soul-searching, I sketched out the rapid evolution of ecocriticism since the term was coined in 1978, pointing to the first-wave emphasis on wildness and wilderness, the second-wave embrace of urban environmental experience and multiculturalism, the third-wave attention to environmental justice and international comparative approaches, and the current fourth wave with its applications to material culture and practical issues of sustainability.

The themes I had begun to notice in presentations at the symposium by the time it was my turn to speak included the recognition and analysis of science as a way of knowing the world, both celebrating science and calling some of its assumptions into question. Our presentations encompassed, as well, the two major paradigms of environmental literature—place and animality—in demonstrating the fundamental role of geography in human experience throughout history and in pointing to the role of art, such as the spiritual music of poetry, in helping us understand our emotional attachments to other species.

At the dawn of Cuban-American collaborations in the Environmental Humanities, represented by a special cluster on Cuban ecotheater that appeared in the Fall 2015 issue of the journal *ISLE*, by our December 2016 gathering in Havana, and by the present volume, I find myself wondering what we can all do to support the international movement of environmental writers and artists. What can American writers do to encourage and support our friends in Cuba? What can Cuban writers do to support us in America as we continue to navigate a dark and confusing time in our own political and cultural history; a time of unprecedented self-interest and corruption? During our symposium in Havana, we were poised at a moment when Cuba seemed to be opening up to environmental thinkers from the rest of the world and the United States was teetering on the verge of isolationism and political extremism.

After I had expressed my Trumpian Angst, Armando Fernandez, the leader of the Cuban contingent at our small meeting, smiled and reassured me that everything would work itself out. There was something wonderful and surreal about being talked down from an existential ledge by someone from a country that had been controlled by a dictatorial regime for more than half a century. So I took heart in the kind words of my new compadre and the eloquence and good humor of my merry band of eco-expats. We amused ourselves during the hours that followed by gazing at the dazzling erratic movements of Havana's butterflies at the *Mariposario*, a team of American nature lovers blown off course by politics. We feasted on flan and, emboldened by rum, strolled through evening boulevards, past statues of great leaders we'd never heard of. The United States seemed so far away, the future both unreal and inevitable. We would soon return to our North American homes, ready to fight the good fight another day. But we now realized that Cuba existed, and we had friends there. We were not alone.

Index

About the Contributors

Susan Bender, who completed her Ph.D. in environmental policy at the University of Nevada, Reno, served most recently as the Senior Director of Global Affairs at the University of California at Irvine. A specialist in international education, she also has interests in environmental literature, population studies, and immigration policy. Before moving to Irvine, she served as senior international officer at the University of Idaho and the University of Nevada, Reno.

Alison Hawthorne Deming's most recent nonfiction book is *Zoologies: On Animals and the Human Spirit* (2014). She is the author of three additional nonfiction books and five poetry books, including most recently *Stairway to Heaven* (2016). *Death Valley: Painted Light*, in collaboration with astronomer/photographer Stephen Strom, also appeared in 2016. Her first book *Science and Other Poems* won the Walt Whitman Award of the Academy of American Poets. The recipient of a 2015 Guggenheim Fellowship, she has also received fellowships from the Fine Arts Work Center, the National Endowment for the Arts, and the Wallace Stegner Fellowship at Stanford University, among other honors. The former Director of the University of Arizona Poetry Center, she is Agnese Nelms Haury Chair in Environment and Social Justice and professor in Creative Writing at the University of Arizona. She lives in Tucson, Arizona, and Grand Manan, New Brunswick, Canada.

Blas Falconer is the author of three poetry collections, *Forgive the Body This Failure* (2018), *The Foundling Wheel* (2012), *A Question of Gravity and Light* (2007), and coeditor of two essay collections, *The Other Latin@: Writing against a Singular Identity* (2011) and *Mentor and Muse: Essays from*

Poets to Poets (2010). The recipient of an NEA Fellowship, the Maureen Egen Writers Exchange, and a Tennessee Individual Artist Grant, his poems have appeared in various literary journals, including *Poetry, Poetry Northwest*, and *Puerto del Sol*. He is the poetry editor for *The Los Angeles Review* and teaches in the low-residency MFA at Murray State University.

Heriberto Feraudy Espino is a writer, researcher, and Africanist, who studied public administration and political science at the University of Havana. He has spent more than thirty years in the field of African studies. Heriberto has been Director of Africa and Middle East in the Cuban Institute of Friendship with the Peoples; Deputy Director of Sub-Saharan Africa in the Ministry of Foreign Affairs of Cuba; and Ambassador of the Republic of Cuba to the Republic of Zambia, the Republic of Botswana, the Federal Republic of Nigeria, the Republic of Mozambique, and the Kingdom of Lesotho. He has also served as a consultant to the United Nations Convention to Combat Desertification and Drought. Among his works are: "Yoruba. An approach to our roots" (essay); Macua (memoir); Irna (memoir); *Fabulous Fables* (children's storybook); *Fables of Lord Turtle* (children's storybook); Of the *Africanía in Cuba. El Ifaismo* (memoir); *La Venus Lukumi* (story); *Simply Nisia* (memoir); *I saw the music* (About the life of Harold Gramatges); "Africa in Memory" (essay); "Racism in Cuba?" (memoir).

Armando Fernandez Soriano is the coordinator for ecological politics for the La Fundación Antonio Núñez Jiménez de la Naturaleza y el Hombre in Cuba. He has served as program coordinator for Caribbean Islands for Coordinadora Regional de Investigaciones Económicas y Sociales (CRIES). He also edited a Cuban scholarly journal, *ILE, anuario de Ecología Cultura y Sociedad*, dedicated to the study of ecology through the lens of culture and society.

Christina Maria Garcia is assistant professor of Spanish and Latin American and Caribbean Studies at the College of Charleston. Her research looks at both literary and visual works from the Hispanophone Caribbean, drawing largely from ecocritical methods of formal analysis. She considers how particular aesthetic techniques can provide alternative forms of imagining the physical body and its environment. Additionally, her work analyzes the elaboration of friendship and hospitality in contemporary Latin American and Caribbean cultural production as a means of unsettling national, heteronormative, and anthropocentric forms of identity.

George B. Handley is associate dean of the College of Humanities, Comparative Arts & Letters at Brigham Young University. Previously he served as chair of the Department of Humanities, Classics, and Comparative Literature. Trained in comparative literature with a focus on literatures of the Americas, he is the author of such books as *New World Poetics: Nature and the Adamic Imagination of Whitman, Neruda, and Walcott* (2007) and coeditor of *Caribbean Literature and the Environment* (2005) and *Postcolonial Ecologies* (2011). He is currently working on a book titled *From Chaos to Cosmos: Literature as Ecotheology*.

Gabriel Horowitz teaches in the Department of World Languages and Cultures at Arkansas State University. He is the author of "The Natural History of Latin American Independence" in *CR: The New Centennial Review*, as well as the chapter "Paraguayan Realism as Cruelty in Gabriel Casaccia's El guajhú" in *Authoritarianism, Cultural History and Political Resistance in Latin America: Exposing Paraguay*.

Mayra Beatriz Martínez is an essayist, columnist, and professor in Havana, Cuba. The dominant focus of her work is José Martí's body of work: travel narratives, stereotypes of the period, and relations with and visions of indigenous and disempowered ethnic groups. She is the author of seven books, including *Martí y los pueblos mayas* (2015) and *Martí ante la danza* (2014), and has won multiple national awards in Cuba for her essays and scholarship.

Margarita Mateo Palmer (Havana, 1950) is an essayist, narrator, and teacher. She has a Ph.D. in literary sciences from the University of Havana and is a member of the Cuban Academy of the Language. Among her most important works are: "Bard Who Sings to You" (1988, essay), "She Wrote Post-criticism" (1995, essay), "Paradiso: The Mythical Adventure" (Alejo Carpentier Prize, 2002, essay), "The Palace of the Pavorreal: The Mythical Voyage" (Enrique Jose Varona of the UNEAC, 2006, essay), "From the White Asylums" (Prize Alejo Carpentier, 2008, novel), "The Mystery of the Echo" (2011, essay), and "Dame the Seven, Theban. The Prose of Antón Arrufat" (Enrique José Varona Prize, 1914, essay). She has won the National Prize for Literary Criticism seven times. She was awarded the National Prize for Literature in 2016.

Karina Pino Gallardo completed her B.A. in theatrology at the University of Arts (ISA) in Havana in 2010. Previously she studied acting at the National Theatre School, from which she graduated in 2003, and she attended the Faculty of Audiovisual Art of Superior Institute of Art in Havana for two years. She works as an editor, critic, and researcher at Tablas-Alarcos Publishing House (and is a founding member of the Editorial area of the Ibero-American Community Theatre and Teaching Unit, University of the Arts).

Biologist, writer, and Guggenheim Fellow **Robert Michael Pyle** has published more than twenty books, including *Wintergreen* (John Burroughs Medal), *Sky*

Time in Gray's River (National Outdoor Book Award), *Evolution of the Genus Iris: Poems*, and a number of standard works on butterflies. He holds a Ph.D. in ecology and environmental studies from Yale University and has taught both natural history and place-based writing in many settings, such as the Aga Khan Trust for Humanities in Tajikistan, workshops from Hobart to Breadloaf, and as Kittredge Distinguished Writer at the University of Montana. A leading lepidopterist, he founded the Xerces Society for Invertebrate Conservation and has been named an Honorary Fellow of the Royal Entomological Society. He is currently collaborating with musician Krist Novoselic on recordings of original compositions for poet and acoustic guitar.

Laura Ruíz Montes is a poet, editor, essayist, and translator. She has published several books of poetry among which are *Written Fall* (1988), *The Shadow of the Others* (1994), *The Road on the Waters* (2004), *To Which Country to Return* (2007), *The Acid Fruits* (2008). As a literary critic, she has published *Another Return to the Native Country* (2012. Prize of the Literary Criticism), *Faith of Errata* (2015), and *Transparencies* (2016). She has also written *A Blind* (theater, 2005), *Today Is Sunday and Tomorrow Also* (children's novel, 2007), and *At the Entrance and Exit* (trial, 2012). In 2017, she published *Slides* (poetry) and a Spanish translation of the novel *The Exile according to Julia* by Gisèle Pineau.

Mariana G. Serra García has a Ph.D. in philological sciences and is a professor in the Faculty of Arts and Letters at the University of Havana, where she has taught Cuban literature and culture for more than three decades. The National Commission for Granting the Scientific Categories of the Ministry of Science, Technology and Environment certified the degree of researcher upon her. She has earned several awards and recognitions: among them, the contest First of January (1975) for her monograph *Reason for Being* (1992) in research project; the Union of Universities of Latin America (UDUAL) in support of research (1994); Annual of the Academy of Sciences of Cuba (2000), and Ibero-American Ethics Award Elena Gil (2004). Her articles and essays have appeared in various Cuban anthologies and magazines and in other countries. She is currently working on a collection of ecocritical essays.

Scott Slovic is professor of literature and environment and professor of natural resources and society at the University of Idaho, where he cofounded the Semester in the Wild Program and teaches environmental writing to a dozen undergraduates each fall semester in the Frank Church River of No Return Wilderness. He served as the founding president of the Association for the Study of Literature and Environment from 1992 to 1995, and since 1995 he has edited *ISLE: Interdisciplinary Studies in Literature and Environment*.

The author, editor, or coeditor of twenty-seven books, his recent publications include *Ecocriticism of the Global South* (2015), *Numbers and Nerves: Information, Emotion, and Meaning in a World of Data* (2015), *Ecocritical Aesthetics: Language, Beauty, and the Environment* (2018), and *The Routledge Handbook of Ecocriticism and Environmental Communication* (2019).

David Taylor is an assistant professor of environmental humanities in the sustainability program at Stony Brook University. His writing crosses disciplinary boundaries and genres—poetry, creative nonfiction, scholarship, and science/technical writing. However, at the core of his work always is the concern for environmental sustainability and community. He is the author and editor of seven books. David has traveled to Cuba for over five years collaborating with writers, artists, and scholars at the University of Havana, Artes Escencias Cubanas, UNEAC (Cuban national writers organization), and the Jimenez Foundation for Sustainability.

Sylvia Torti is a biologist and writer. She received her doctorate in biology by conducting studies on diversity in tropical forests in Africa and Central America. In her short stories and novels she is interested in the interaction between scientists and the subjects they study. In 2005, her novel *The Scorpion's Tail* won the Miguel Marmól Award for the first work as an American of Latino descent. This work was inspired by personal experiences when she witnessed the Zapatista uprising while conducting field studies in Chiapas, Mexico. Her current novel, *Cages*, takes place in a laboratory, where the songs of birds are studied, and it explores the limits of learned language, communication, and memory. Torti is currently Dean of Honors College at the University of Utah. From 2009 to 2012, she was associate director of the Rio Mesa Center, an interdiciplinary field center on the Colorado Plateau. She is codirector of the interdisciplinary workshop "Mapping Meaning" (www.mappingmeaning.org) that takes place every two years in the field.

www.ingramcontent.com/pod-product-compliance
Lightning Source LLC
LaVergne TN
LVHW011519200926
848484LV00001B/81